OUR SELVES UNKNOWN

BY THE SAME AUTHOR:

HOUSES

THE WORLD OF ARCHITECTURE

LANDSCAPE IN DISTRESS

PARAMETERS AND IMAGES

THE SHELL GUIDE TO NORTH WALES
(with E. Beasley)

ANOTHER VERSION
(poems)

A BROKEN WAVE:
The Rebuilding of England 1940–1980

THE CONTINUING HERITAGE

OUR SELVES UNKNOWN

An Autobiography

by

LIONEL BRETT

We that acquaint ourselves with ev'ry ZOANE
And passe both TROPIKES and behold the POLES,
When we come home are to our selves unknown
And unacquainted still with our own SOULES.

Alexander Pope

LONDON
VICTOR GOLLANCZ LTD
1985

First published in Great Britain 1985
by Victor Gollancz Ltd,
14 Henrietta Street, London WC2E 8QJ

© Lionel Brett 1985

British Library Cataloguing in Publication Data
Esher, Lionel Brett, *Viscount*
   Our selves unknown: an autobiography.
   1. Esher, Lionel Brett, *Viscount*
   2. Architects—Great Britain—Biography
   I. Title
   720'.92'4   NA997.E8

   ISBN 0–575–03552–8

Typeset at The Spartan Press Limited, Lymington, Hants
and printed in Great Britain by
St Edmundsbury Press, Bury St Edmunds, Suffolk
Illustrations originated and printed by Thomas Campone, Southampton

To those who died

ACKNOWLEDGEMENTS

The lines by Siegfried Sassoon on page 56 are from *The Heart's Journey* (1928) and are reprinted by permission of the publisher William Heinemann Ltd; those by John Masefield on page 68 first appeared in *The Times* in 1938 and are reprinted by permission of The Society of Authors as the literary representative of the Estate of John Masefield; those by E. M. Forster on page 153 are reprinted by permission of The Society of Authors as the literary representative of the Estate of E. M. Forster; those by Laurens van der Post on page 183 are from *The Dark Eye in Africa* and are reprinted by kind permission of the author and The Hogarth Press.

CONTENTS

LIST OF ILLUSTRATIONS

OUR SELVES UNKNOWN

Chapter one

GRANDFATHERS

"HE'S DELICATE, YOU know," said Nurse Turner, hoisting me into the tall coachbuilt pram where lay the sleeping bundle of my sister Jinny. (I was not, of course: this was a conversational gambit. But it was nice to get a lift.) From this vantage point, as we glided slowly northward under the vast canopy of London planes, I could survey the dullish scene. Below the shabby bow-fronted houses of Park Lane the sparse traffic was equally shabby — a few taxis with gas bags on their roofs, a few carts and drays, and a lot of solid-tyred open-topped buses in various liveries. It produced, considering its low density and low speed, a considerable clatter and cacophony, contributing to the background roar which was already the bass note of London life. Somewhere short of Marble Arch we generally turned back, downhill all the way, crossed the street under the bobby's arm at Hyde Park Corner, and sped past the main entrance of St George's Hospital. In and out passed spectacularly wounded officers, an enthralling spectacle. Grosvenor Crescent was often "up" (under repair), no doubt for the insertion of new gas or electric mains, and we would stop and watch a sledgehammer gang in perfect rhythm hit the nail on the head. Streets, being all paved with tarred wood blocks, came up quite easily.

Occasionally a stretch covered with straw indicated a serious illness in one of the tall Belgravian houses, whose stucco fronts in a variety of colours from battleship grey to buttercup yellow now peeled from wartime neglect. Our own house in Upper Belgrave Street was unusual in being detached and only three storeys high, but though recently built it was draughty, and on winter evenings, when the wind moaned under the drawing-room door during the children's hour, "that", my father would say, "is the Beastly Bear of Belgrave Square".

He had a job in the War Office, being spared active service, he later told me, on account of his flat feet. There he shared a room and a lot of fun with the amiable and clever Charlotte Ogilvy, still around in the 1980s as Lady Bonham Carter, gallantly riding the bus to every art-world soirée in town.

"The Parents" (sub-species of the Groans, which embraced all grown-up house guests but not the servants, who were individual personalities never so categorized by us) practised a not uncommon division of labour. He ran the fun side, she the discipline. This was hard on her, particularly since her New England upbringing made her take it seriously. Manners, competitiveness, stoicism, accuracy — these were the Four Virtues. ("Have you no manners, Lionel?" "Yes, I've got them, but I'm not using them." My mother recorded this exchange.) The traditional agents for inculcating these virtues were governesses, primarily French ones, to whom they came more naturally than to the Germans, who were apt to be sentimental. Mim, from the dreary Pas de Calais, was elegant, pasty-faced, large-eyed, and so dedicated a disciplinarian that she once entered into a tug-of-war, with myself the rope, when my father proposed to break some rule. But I loved her, and through the first prep-school nights it was for her I wept. Frauly, her German successor, cheery, round-faced, tow-haired, was a soft touch and mercilessly ragged by my three sisters.

In the nursery world, dedicated in any case to plain living, the war had very little impact: in that pre-plastic and pre-electronic age children didn't have much in the way of toys, and books were always a higher family priority. Guns, tanks and soldiers were banned by my father as militaristic. On nights of Zeppelin raids we staggered down to the basement where we slept on the green baize shelves of a large silver safe with an iron door. But Teddy Tail of the *Daily Mail* and Pip, Squeak and Wilfred of the *Daily Mirror* were more real to us than the Kaiser and his generals. As a Liberal and pro-Boer, my father, while not actually pro-German, which was impossible, was severely anti anti-German and discouraged the cruder forms of propaganda. The real bogey man in nursery circles was the Bolshie, caricatured as a hirsute creature with a smoking bomb concealed behind his back. We were intensely patriotic. *Our Island Story*, our first history book, convinced us how incredibly lucky we were to be English, or alternatively American. My American aunt gave me a silver mug with figures of children in various ethnic costumes and the inscription:

Little Indian, Sioux or Crow, little frosty Eskimo,
Little Turk or Japanee, oh don't you wish that you were me?

My first words, appropriately enough for a member of my generation, were "Oh dear", and I look at the snapshot photographer with a wary eye. The stereotype of the stable and immutable English nanny did not apply in my case, the turnover rate in our nursery being exceptionally high, with nine coming and going in my first six years. At that point one was promoted to the school-room — a class of half a dozen others taught by a visiting spinster. There was a rigid marking system, and being on home ground I was always top, so that it became a family rule that I should be top of everything. Afternoons, there would be singing or dancing classes, a gymnasium in Sloane Street and Smith's horrible riding school, stinking of horses, where we rode round a ring like circus trainees. Bicycling round Belgrave Square seemed to me an infinitely more civilized form of transportation, and after being heavily thrown in Hyde Park I was allowed to give up riding for good. Ponies were for girls.

My mother's relations with her family had never been cosy, and as America moved into the Jazz Age she was to feel less and less at home there. But for the first few years of her married life, with my father's English friends scattered by the war and his parents less than welcoming, she crossed the Atlantic a good deal. When I was only a few months old we went over in the *Lusitania*, spent Christmas and returned on some German ship a few months before the war started. We went again a couple of summers later at the height of the U-boat campaign, sailing from Liverpool and landing at Halifax, Nova Scotia. Thereafter, through the twenties, we made the trip every two or three years, trying a different liner each time, from the slow but steady *Homeric* to the speedy *Aquitania* and *Olympic*. Once we tried the St Lawrence iceberg route in the rocky little *Empress of France*, and once we travelled grandly in the enormous ex-German *Majestic*. But whichever the ship or the line, the routine never varied: chicken broth at eleven under a tartan rug on B deck, reclining on slatted chairs in a windblown family line then, at noon, announced by a gut-shaking blast on the great siren, the sweepstake on the day's run, in which we each had a ticket. After the huge lunch, shuffleboard and deck-tennis ("Why not ask that nice-looking boy to make a four?"). Teacakes to palm lounge music, then a long read, my eyes too full of tears to make out the print of the Everyman *Last of the Mohicans*. We were lucky that these journeys coincided with the great days of the Atlantic liner trade, with film stars and millionaires to stare at, returning soldiers or emigrants in the hold, and with the great days of the arrival in New York, while Manhattan was still a magic water-borne cluster of the tallest towers and spires in the world, wreathed in the smoke and echoing the sirens of ships of all sizes. The World Trade Center, visually the most disastrous building in the world, has now destroyed that silhouette for ever. In our lifetimes all these immense ships, whose pink or yellow funnels towered high above the elms and mud flats of Southampton Water, were to disappear entirely, and with them the drama of departure, with the little knot of waving spectators at the pier end, as the gap of water widened between them and those they could no longer speak to and could hardly see, and the drama of arrival at the feet of the skyscrapers in the midst of the heedless shuttling traffic of the West Side Drive.

My grandfather's Lincoln would be on the dockside, and would whisk us straight down to "Wincoma", their Kensington-Italianate stucco mansion on the fringe of Huntington, Long Island. It was surrounded by a spacious porch with a shiny wooden floor ideal for children's vehicles. The interior, guarded by a sinister English butler called Trapp, was Victorian and, like all American houses in summer, deeply shaded. It contained appropriate artworks of clippers in full sail or woods at sunset, and my parents, whose taste was moving from Chippendale towards Regency, thought it perfectly hideous. Watered lawns stretched out vaguely under assorted conifers, and at the end of the garden there was a secluded fly-screened bungalow full of children's junk. Close by, a range of garages displayed half a dozen highly variegated motor cars whose shiny brass or lacquered bonnets were carefully lined up a couple of feet forward of the garage doors. A path through long grass hissing with crickets and katydids led down to the jetty, built of marvellously wind-blasted timbers, where lay my grandfather's new-fangled orange and black motor yacht. This was a come-down from the great days of the *Anahma*, his graceful white schooner-prowed steam yacht with tall yellow funnel, which he had had to sell in the war. Alongside was a small beach, lapped by the smoothly shining waters of Long Island Sound, and scattered in its sand were large round granite boulders, among which lurked horseshoe crabs, frighteningly large but harmless creatures of primeval aspect descended to us from remote eons of time. From this ageless scene my grandfather commuted rapidly into New York, and here in the evenings, before swimming pools had come in, he bathed.

Mr Heckscher was the younger son of a distinguished *hochbürgerlich* family of Hamburg. His father had fought against Napoleon in the three-day battle of Leipzig in 1813 and his uncle had been in Wellington's army at Waterloo. In 1848, the year of my grandfather's birth, his father, a successful lawyer in his fifties, became a Liberal representative of the free city of Hamburg in the abortive Frankfurt Parliament and subsequently its Prime Minister. When militant students turned against this ineffective body my great-grandfather was practically murdered (Prince Lichnowski, who sat beside him in his carriage, was killed), but he talked down the mob with great courage. Scenes such as this led to the savage Prussian repression, to which he was bitterly opposed. He returned, disillusioned, to Hamburg and ended his days rather sadly as the city's ambassador in Vienna.

In 1867, soon after his father died, young August Heckscher set out across the Atlantic, with 500 dollars in gold strapped around his waist. Through some family connection he got a job in a coal mine in Pennsylvania, and before long found himself its manager through a period of violent industrial strife. He stuck it out for ten years until the mine closed down in 1881. By then he felt sufficiently established to get married to one Nanny Atkins of Pottsville, Pennsylvania, a buxom, smiling girl whose family had been established in the state since the eighteenth century. Conventional, uncomplicated, perhaps slightly snobbish (she always called him Auguste with an "e" on the end, as though he were French, and she gave both her children French names, Maurice and Antoinette), she seems to have given my grandfather the firm base and the emotional security he needed. For he now developed as an entrepreneur of astonishing versatility. He bought control of a bankrupt zinc plant in New Jersey and resurrected it so rapidly that he ran into opposition from vested interests in the industry who decided to fight his title for the business. There followed a legal battle which lasted for ten years, during which he took the case from court to court, travelled the world to collect evidence and finally persuaded the Appeals Court to reverse its verdict. ("Halcyon days," he later called this period in a letter to my mother.) In 1890, in the midst of this, his bank collapsed in the wake of the Baring Brothers' collapse in London, and he found himself overnight reduced to total penury. He borrowed from friends, fought on and gradually re-established himself. "I am not impatient," he said, "I have been blessed with a faculty for perseverance no matter what happens. I do not give in." But he was incapable of resting on his laurels. He searched for other bankrupt businesses he could rehabilitate. He was appointed by the Courts to the receivership of several railroads in Kansas and of a large steel plant in New Jersey. He built fire engines and sold them to several state governments; he took over a copper mine in Utah, sugar plantations in Cuba and planted 50,000 orange trees in Florida. In each case he applied himself with his extraordinary assiduity to learning minute detail about each new industry: thoroughness was always his strong suit, though as he grew older his intuitions became more erratic. Occasionally he fell among crooks, and in old age he became rather paranoiac about this. He himself was, I believe, entirely honest.

In the twenty years over which I knew him my grandfather was a small, unbending, agile man with steel spectacles and a neat grey beard. He treated both his children with great generosity, and at monthly intervals dictated to one or other of my parents a dignified and not unfeeling letter from his office on East 42nd Street. But his son was a tragedy. Extremely good-looking and athletic, he had married a warm-hearted, funny, blessedly un-intellectual girl and with her produced four children, my first cousins, all of whom were outstandingly intelligent. For some years after the war, they had lived a life of Fitzgeraldean glamour in their large country house at Westbury in a landscape as lush and pastoral as the Surrey of the 1890s. All were splendid riders, swimmers, golfers; we felt pale and weedy beside them. But in the mid-1920s Maurice had already begun to womanize and gamble. My aunt Louise stuck it out for a few years, then in 1926 divorced him. Westbury was sold and she moved to a modest wooden house she appropriately called Shadows End. His life thereafter became a rake's progress of drink and bankruptcies and failed marriages, redeemed at the end by a devoted last wife.

In 1924 my grandmother, ailing from some mysterious disease and for the first time nervous of the future, paid her first and only visit to my parents in England. She did not survive the voyage home. Deprived of her restraining hand, my grandfather plunged more ardently into business adventures. He moved out of industry into real estate, first in Florida and then in New York. He built a small skyscraper (only 24 storeys) on Fifth Avenue close to the southern end of Central Park, classical in design with a golden cock atop its pyramidal roof. But unluckily the Rockefellers, with their vastly greater resources, moved into the same area with their colossal Radio City development, into which, by methods which he considered contemptible, they were able to lure a great many of his tenants. But he fought back: "We are working hard from day to day patching up difficult situations at considerable cost, but I am very fond of hard work and not the least bit dismayed." Increasingly, as the twenties wore on, he was able to collect resources for charitable activities — two playgrounds in Central Park, others in slum areas of Manhattan, a holiday home for poor children on Long Island, a public park for his village of Huntington containing an art gallery into which he moved some of the grander pieces from Wincoma, of which the centrepiece was a fountain featuring three sentimental nude children — my two sisters and myself. He basked in the good opinions which these activities brought him: "We had the most wonderful reception and homecoming festivities on Wednesday last. Practically the entire village paraded, stores were closed, the children had a fête day and our Long Island friends, who as a rule have not that reputation, went to very large expense to welcome us back to Huntington. It was touching and inspiring, and coming as it does at the end of a long and rather busy life, in the midst of strife and people here who ought to be decent and generous, but are small and contemptible, it was a refreshing counter-experience." Central to all was the Heckscher Foundation for Children on Vanderbilt Avenue, a main preoccupation of his later years.

In 1930, after an embarrassing episode with an opera singer which cost him a certain amount of money, he married a large lady "of English parentage and wealthy, as I understand it, in her own right". In fact, she was generally thought to be after his money, but she never got it: he got a great deal of hers for his Foundation. But to the horror of my cousins, she turned out after the death of both of them to have had a number of children in Texas who laid claim to his by then quite small estate and had to be fought off in the Courts. The great Depression, which drove many of his friends to suicide, he found exhilarating: "You can take for granted that the strain has been terrific and I am rather surprised at myself, since I am familiar with all the details and still directing matters generally, to find myself standing up rather joyously under the load," he wrote at the age of eighty-seven. "I am striking my gait again, I am glad to say, and feel now the lilt of business, which I always experience when we do not fall down on everything that we attempt." In that same letter to my mother he reported on one of his talks with F. D. Roosevelt, whom he considered "has made a better President of the United States than anyone I can recollect — and I have known them pretty much all since Lincoln. Even Lincoln could not have faced the present situation with the surprising equanimity and resourcefulness shown by the crippled President in Washington". But he was not unscathed. In 1932 he had a nervous collapse and began to feel himself to be surrounded by crooks and time-servers. He soon revised his opinion of Roosevelt: "Matters in this country are not mending at all. Our President of the golden tongue is utterly untrustworthy and has set the country by the ears." At ninety the dark side of New York was uppermost in his mind: "The Heckscher Foundation is in bad case because the population there is completely changed and is actually now in that vicinity a haven for cutthroats, thieves and racketeers. Even the mothers are tainted and the children from eight and nine years up are completely out of bounds and actually conceal knives and pistols. Even the policemen travel in pairs and fours after dark. You would not believe such a state of affairs could endure in a city like New York, but it does in fact endure and we are doing our best to sell the Foundation building and get out from under. We are not giving each other presents. We are too poor." It was as well that he died in 1940, since he naturally had a good deal of sympathy for the Germans, deeply disliked the French and would have been horrified at America's involvement in the war.

For us children, far and away his most glamorous possession was the Camp which he had built, largely for our benefit, on the shores of Little Moose Lake in the Adirondacks. This was a vast tract of virgin wilderness owned by a syndicate of which he was a member. It was granite country, overlaid by peat, with small rounded mountains and innumerable lakes of all sizes, many of them formed by beaver dams and linked by tumbling rivers, the whole clothed in primeval forest. Motor cars, motor boats, hunting and every other kind of exploitation were prohibited, so that moose, bear, porcupine and an infinite variety of smaller creatures abounded. We would take the night train from New York to the little forest village of Old Forge and thence travel by dirt road to the clubhouse and general store at the lake-head. There Ben and William would be waiting with the guide boats. These were two Whitmanesque pioneers, Ben shy and taciturn, William cosier and a story-teller. They had built the boats themselves, and they were unique craft, as graceful as gondolas and like gondolas lacquered black outside, with black oars; inside, one was a glossy maroon colour, the other a dark green. They were so precious that we were never allowed to row them. Thus, deeply laden, the two guides ferried us across, a row of fifteen minutes or so, and docked us under my grandfather's chalet-like boathouse, built among smooth dome-shaped rocks that plunged sharply into the peaty water. The house itself, a ramshackle, shingled affair, roadless and gardenless, was built on the ridge of a little peninsula so that it was almost entirely surrounded by water. Boardwalks, ideal for the vehicles of our smaller siblings, led up from the boathouse and radiated to ancillary buildings, and only a few shafts of sunlight penetrated the forest canopy all around. There we pale English children confronted our American cousins, blond and brown in their denim overalls, and in this backwood setting had much the worst of it. But who cared! We were out of this world. Small wooded mountains stood around the lake, and beyond them more lakes, creeks and wooded mountains stretched, as far as we knew, to the Arctic Circle.

My four cousins were generally already there. Bunnie, the oldest girl, serious and romantic, who all her life was to remind people of Charlotte Brontë, Nancy with naughty marmoset face and uncontrollable hair, Augie, my contemporary and lifelong friend, and Maurie, the youngest, idealistic, sensitive, insecure, and as good-looking as the father with whom he had absolutely nothing in common. Within a day or two, my father, prime mover in all expeditions, would announce plans for our first venture into the wilderness. "How jolly ripping!" I would exclaim, to ribaldry from my cousins. The two guides laden with provisions, we would plod off in Indian file, each with a basket-work back-pack to suit his size. After an hour or so the trail would end at a lakeside, and here flat-bottomed row boats would be waiting in which we would transport ourselves to the other end of the lake and pick up the trail again. Marked by blazes on the boles of ancient trees it would cross streams by plank bridges or zig-zag up forested mountains with bare granite tops. Towards sunset, if things had worked out right, we would reach the camp we had booked for the night, a small shack generally by the side of some lake and containing blankets and cooking utensils. We would swim in the dark water among ghostly trees killed by the activities of beavers, then build a great camp fire to last the night. The guides would produce a terrific fry-up followed by flapjacks in maple syrup, then we would sleep in a circle with our feet to the fire. In the small hours, under the moon, one of us would get up to scare a porcupine rummaging in the trash can and to throw a log on the fire, in the glare of which we would see pairs of eyes, at different levels, watching us out of the total blackness of the surrounding forest. Occasionally we would hear the melancholy cry of a loon winging its way across the misty waters.

Other summers, we would take the Night Scot from Euston, change at Stirling on to the old Caledonian line and arrive for breakfast at Callander. An inconspicuous entry off the long main street of that dour granite town led to my other grandfather's beloved pink harled house, known as the Roman Camp because of the remains in a paddock alongside of a square second-century vallum. The nucleus of the house, rarely for Scotland, is a modest sixteenth-century manor house, which my grandfather, who had bought it in 1897, had extended rather well, with low wings and slate pepper-pot roofs. At the end of the lawn was the wide tumbling Teith, a salmon river noted for its pearls, and to the north, over beds of phloxes, could at times be seen the blue or slate grey peak of Ben Ledi, most of which, with another moor to the east, belonged to my grandfather. Callander, ever since the Victorian invasion of Scotland, had called itself the Gateway to the Highlands, and in summer, even in the twenties, enough char-a-bancs passed through on the way to the Trossachs or via the Pass of Leny to Lochearnhead to support the Pedlar's Pack, a "horror shop" (in my parents' phrase), where my grandmother, no doubt to fill the days of her husband's absence on royal or political business, sold knicknacks to tourists (and to us) in a hut on the Doune road. Wide open to the south and west, sheltered from the north by the wall of the Highlands, Callander always seemed to us searchlit by the westering sun.

Relations with my Brett cousins were jollier than with my Heckscher ones, for we shared school slang and also shared an ugly villa on the High Street, the Bairns' House, where, sketchily chaperoned sometimes by some dim tutor or governess, we got right away from anxious parental or alarming grandparental control. I never felt a twinge of jealousy of the fact that my contemporary Tony was angelically good-looking and obviously my grandfather's favourite. "Posh style", he would generously say as I "addressed the ball" on Callander's nine-hole golf course and then missed it. His two sisters were equally matey and laughed at my jokes.

We had a wonderful pillow-fight all afternoon [my diary records]: "Ange + Mar v Jinny and I. [Next day] the Groans away for the day. At breakfast Grandma had an idea. Marie, Jinny and I were to try and be absolutely *perfect* for the day, for which we were to receive prizes. Angela was judge. We spent all morning being polite to each other while it rained. After lunch we bought lollipops in the town, then went to the Bracklin Falls. The Groans came back at seven. Grandma then gave out the prizes. I got First . . . [needless to say].

But the "days on the hill" were the great days. After an earlier breakfast (in Scotland, my father insisted, one should always stand to eat porridge) there would be the usual excited assemblage of eccentric vehicles, of which my grandfather's Metallurgique with its brass serpent horn was the star, and Alfie, the old coachman's son, the driver, ponies, shivering spaniels, girls in tartan (dubiously justified by my grandfather's Forbes great-grandmother), my father and his brother and all the ghillies and male staff in a tweed specially woven for my grandfather in Killin. The convoy would then set forth, climb perhaps the steep and gloomy Stank Glen, with its shadowed cascade, beside which my grandfather had lately built a little mausoleum to contain his ashes. Deployed by Willie McLeod, the keeper, we would then walk all day for a mixed bag of grouse, hares, ptarmigan, blackgame and rabbits, eating our sandwiches perhaps on Ardnandave Hill with its steep view into the black depths of Loch Lubnaig. Even this modest elevation was inscribed on one of the collection of walking sticks on which my father recorded the name of every hill he climbed — the origin, perhaps, of my own passion for getting to the tops of mountains. But Ben Ledi itself had the feel of a real peak with its sharpish ridge overhanging a grim crater-like corrie. From the cairn one looked north to the Braes of Balquhidder and the country of Rob Roy, the Scottish Robin Hood, familiar to us all from our dutiful reading of Walter Scott, most of whose novels I managed to get through before I went to school. Like all converts my grandfather and his sons were passionately addicted to Scottish mythology. Their reputed descent from John Baliol, the puppet King of Scotland in 1292, was a slight embarrassment, though it need not have been; Baliol, I have now been told, was no more of a Norman than Robert the Bruce.

On these days my grandfather only appeared briefly on a pony. He was away a good deal, having, it was said, originally bought the place because it was an easy day's drive from Balmoral. (He had built a "Tudorbethan" house in Windsor Forest, in which I was born, for the same reason.) But even in his absence his formidable personality haunted the place. The garden was full of crossed E's, ornaments attesting to his romantic taste, including the pretty Bothy by the river bank, where as a young girl Aunt Doll had set up her studio. His library, darkly panelled and lined with his portentously secret correspondence, was out of bounds at all times. When he was at home we were, of course, on our best behaviour and somewhat *exalté*. In the low-ceilinged dining-room, with carved Renaissance chimney piece and Jacobean chairs, where the tipsy butler and our friend Alfred the handsome footman waited at table wearing their Great War medal ribbons, my grandfather, his charm, irony and authority as imposing as ever, held court as he always had.

Reggie Brett had been born in 1852, the elder son of a great Victorian judge, the first Master of the Rolls since Coke to be given a Viscounty. The Bretts were Home Counties gentry, Jane Austen characters, Indian Army officers or philoprogenitive clergymen. Baliol Brett, son of one such, had not particularly distinguished himself except as Captain of the Cambridge crew which beat Oxford in 1839. An easy-going and ambitious law student,

> . . . his determination to succeed [according to my father's account] was the creation of his deep and life-long love for his beautiful French wife. A man of natural simplicity and deep piety, he had no real desire for money or position, except in so far as they pleased the lady of his love. A strong sense of duty kept him rather unwillingly a slave to his laborious days. A tall, handsome man, with a lovely nature, stamped with all the virtues and none of the vices of his Victorian period. All his life she remained the love of his life, writing to her the beautiful letters, some of which have been published in *A Romance of the Nineteenth Century*.

On the foreign and maternal side her heredity is more obscure and more interesting. Her mother's grandfather appears to have been an Alsatian peasant, whose three attractive daughters made some noise in the confused Napoleonic years. One married into the lesser nobility of France; one became the mistress of Dumas; and the third, bringing a daughter with her, appeared in England and married Colonel Gurwood, the aide-de-camp of the Duke of Wellington and the editor of his despatches. Mother and daughter shared an unknown past, calling themselves by the name of Mayer. It was said that the mother had been a *vivandière* and that the daughter had been born on the field of Waterloo. Much was said, but nothing was known. Naturally a punctilious age did not receive such people, and they drifted easily into the Gore House set, where Lady Blessington and Count d'Orsay, living in sin, had surrounded themselves by all the most intelligent and attractive men in London, but where no respectable woman set foot. Even her mother's marriage to Colonel Gurwood was not sufficient to overcome her doubtful past and the lugubrious and discontented soldier took care to leave her at home when he went into Society.

There is no doubt that this treatment entered like iron into the cold French soul of the beautiful daughter. With no position and no money she did not find it easy to marry, and she was approaching thirty when the ardent and unknown lawyer laid at her feet the exquisite gift of his devotion. She accepted it grudgingly, but during the long years to follow melted and grew to love him. Nevertheless she remained a cold, proud, ambitious woman, very prudish and particular, mean about money, and with a snobbish interest in social position.

For his part he remained uncorrupted by success. "I cannot expect you always to be working well," he wrote to my grandfather at his prep school, "or so as to satisfy Mr Tabor [his headmaster]. I care nothing about all that, so long as he has nothing to say against your honour and goodness."

It would not have been characteristic of my grandfather's ambitious generation to have taken this nobly mid-Victorian advice. Nor would his parents, who sent him to Eton as the foundation of a great career, have been wholly happy if he had. At Eton his charm, wit and good looks caught the eye of William Johnson (William Cory). This remarkable teacher, who left under a cloud a few years later, implanted in his disciples the two complementary ideals of romantic homosexual love and high-minded service to the Empire. The model was classical Greece, the myth that of Achilles and Patroclus. Floating in a dodger on the silent Thames, then at the height of its elmy beauty, friendships were formed which were to last a political lifetime, and in long tutorials radical imperialism acquired its characteristic stamp. To have to leave this hedonist's paradise, even for Cambridge, was heart-rending for my grandfather.

Years later, the recollection reduced him to tears. It seemed a threat to his private life and created a distaste for the public arena that was to be his best-known characteristic. But in the end a conspiracy of his aristocratic patrons (in this case Sir William Harcourt and Lady Ripon) forced him into political life as Private Secretary to Lord Hartington, then leader of the Liberal opposition, and into the strange career which his remarkable talents opened up to him.

The central theme of this career was that as against decadent France and isolationist America only the British Empire could save the liberal values of the West from "Prussianism". As early as 1906, in the apparently cloudless Edwardian summer, he could write to his old friend Millie, Duchess of Sutherland:

> There is a bad time coming for soldiers; for the laws of ethnographic evolution require that we shall fight one of the most powerful military empires that has ever existed. This is *certain*, and we have a very short period of preparation. I fear that proficiency in games, or in the hunting field, will not help our poor lads much when they have to face the carefully trained and highly educated German officers.

The Defence reorganization of 1904, which abolished the Commander-in-Chief, set up the Committee of Imperial Defence (of which he became a permanent member), created the Army Council and thus "solved the vexed problem of dual civilian and professional control", has been described by a recent biographer as "Esher's masterpiece". And a decade later, when the new machinery was duly tested in action, it was he who, working in Paris, held it together, not only as the trusted link between the Government and the Army as the political adviser of Kitchener and Haig, but also as the confidant of the French General Staff and the only effective liaison between the two allied Governments.

He had unique qualifications for these roles. There was his French blood and his command of the language. Then his marriage to the daughter of Sylvain Van der Weyer, the creator of modern Belgium and through the discreet Baron Stockmar an intimate of Queen Victoria, led to his editing her earlier correspondence, his special knowledge of the relationship between Monarch and Prime Minister and his role as the friend and recognized adviser of Edward VII and George V on constitutional and military matters. "You are a wonderful man; everything you touch succeeds," King Edward wrote to him on the success of his Territorial Army recruiting drive in 1909. But he was no mere royal favourite. The secret was to have a foot in every camp. He knew Fleet Street intimately, and long before such techniques were commonplace he was a master of the carefully timed leak and of the inspirational leader. Above all he was the old and trusted friend of Prime Ministers irrespective of party, "on the best of terms with mutual enemies like Chamberlain and Morley, Rosebery and Hartington, Harcourt and Balfour, Asquith and Lloyd George". He had an extraordinary capacity for influencing people; he had curiosity, even into our doings as children, and he was never bored by detail. His state papers, crisp and lucid, still make exhilarating reading.

Yet, as is well known, he consistently refused responsibility. "Power and Place," he coolly observed, "are not synonymous." The most traumatic for him of these refusals was undoubtedly that of the War Office in 1903, when he had not only to stand up to the Prime Minister but also to disappoint and offend the King, which he found much more painful. After that, similar refusals came more easily. Of the Viceroyship of India, offered him by Asquith in 1908, he wrote:

> I said that I was very much honoured, and most grateful, but that I could not give up my work here both with the King and on the Committee of Imperial Defence . . . I am confident that in going to India I should be throwing away the substance of power for the shadow . . . besides everyday questions arise, of vital importance to our country, when I can have my say and can sway a decision. India would be for me (it sounds vain but it is not) parochial.

And of the Paris Embassy, pressed upon him in 1917: "I cannot imagine anything I should detest more."

In a letter to Maurice from Balmoral, in the midst of the struggle to decide whether to enter the Cabinet in 1907, he confesses his attitude to all such offers:

It is not in my line to go back into politics and become identified
with party strife. I can do more good outside, and heavens how
much happier the life. Just imagine what the tie would be. I am
purely selfish in the matter, and really I do not think I can bring
myself to sacrifice all independence, all liberty of action, all my
intime life for a position which adds nothing to that which I now
occupy. Is it not a piece of bad luck that I who loathe "public life"
should be dragged into it? I have walked alone all the afternoon in
the woods and meditated on our quiet, happy, secluded life. I am
sure the War Office would break into the harmony of our lives . . .
the world is nothing to me compared with your love.

The need to be adored can be blamed on egotism or excused as
insecurity, depending whether one looks to the indulgent father or the
censorious mother. Certainly my grandfather never took a chance,
never risked failure, either in his public or his private life. His friends
were always men or women who would look up to him. Nellie Van
der Weyer, the mousey little Belgian whom he married "out of the
schoolroom", was intelligent enough never to bore him, to defer to
his own intelligence, and to know that all her life she would play
Second Fiddle — indeed she so entitled a touching poem. But lovers *de
haut en bas* can create zombies, and it is doubtful whether any of his
élite wholly escaped this fate. Certainly my Uncle Maurice, grossly
spoiled as a child and absurdly flattered as a young man ("there is no
position, however lofty, which you will not some day be qualified to
fill . . . your beloved breast has been broadened by Providence for the
stars which some day will cover it"), fell a victim. He was a decent,
shy, ugly man of no great ability, helplessly hypnotized into jumping
the gun for an A.D.C. appointment and then ignominiously having to
resign his commission in the Coldstream when he married an actress.
In fact, beautiful Zena Dare, herself under the magician's spell, was
the love of his life, and indeed of us all, bringing the fresh air of
generous normality into the family hothouse.

For my two desperate aunts it was too late. Written off from an
early age as plain and tongue-tied, and therefore made so, they
suffered agonies of adolescent inadequacy, followed by brief seasons
as ballroom wallflowers. But they fought their way out. Handsome
blonde Doll, a rebel from the start, became, to her father's fury, the
protégée of the formidable Ranee of Sarawak, who fancied her for her

equally tongue-tied son and heir. But an adolescent shock had put her off marriage and it was her sister, little Syv, who in due course became "Queen of the Headhunters", and the neglected wife of the uncouth and unfaithful last Rajah of that jungle kingdom. Lonely and insecure, Syv soon dropped out of Society into the nightclub circuit; one of her daughters married a band leader, another an all-in-wrestler (the third married a shipping magnate). In her novels and autobiographies she never concealed the malice and jealousy that were the ruin of her early life. Her poison-pen letters about my mother when she first arrived in England were so horrific that my father, who normally kept everything and bound it in red leather, burnt the lot, and described her to me as "a female Iago". Meanwhile, Doll made her getaway to the Slade, befriended the handsome and tragic Mark Gertler, became the crony of the equally tragic Carrington and Katherine Mansfield, had a crush on Lady Ottoline Morell, and in due course (as "Brett") became the adoring confidante of D. H. Lawrence, outliving them all to die in Taos, aged ninety-three. Desperate all her life for cash, which she gave away to hard-up dropouts as soon as she could get it, intermittently rescued by my father or myself ("the brutes can pay" was the Bohemian motto he sardonically attributed to her), she finally triumphed both as artist and as human being. But though she had fought him like a tiger she never escaped the spell of the magician. When she heard that John Rothenstein had chosen two of her pictures for the Tate she exclaimed, "Pupsie must have turned in his urn," and on the garage door of her slummy adobe studio in the sagebrush she had painted the Esher arms seven feet high.

In our days at the Roman Camp my grandfather was living, as he always had, well above his social and financial station and having to borrow from my parents. But of course we saw no sign of this, and scarcely a sign of the feuds that had torn his children apart. My Brett cousins, Maurice and Zena's children, seemed cheerfully unaware of their father's financial anxieties or of his lifetime of abject dependence. The beauty of the place and its romantic associations united us all, and at the centre of it the disillusioned Prospero of this enchanted kingdom never lost his infectious delight in the healing powers of the Highlands.

It is one of those lovely days which you know so well, with only a slight ripple on the loch, and white clouds which throw a shadow over the birches of Ellen's Isle and the brilliant purple heather beyond. We have landed on the slopes of Ben Venue, not quite at the usual place, and after lunch everyone has gone his or her way. I don't suppose that if one wandered thousands of miles south, it would be possible to find a more beautiful spot or a more beautiful sky. We might be on the slopes of Hymettus, or under the shadow of Etna. . . . All the Scottish lore, which generations past and to come breathe in with their childhood, seems to gather round and have its origin in the hills and lochs and burns of the home which is ours. . . . All the happiest days of our very happy life have been lived in the shadow of these hills.

But it too was to dissolve into thin air. Maurice, to whom it was left on my grandfather's death in 1930, survived him by only four years. Double death duties forced a sale; it became a secluded little hotel, and the yards and yards of leather-bound volumes of my grandfather's secret correspondence with his loves and his colleagues, with Kings and Ministers, in which public and private matters were inextricably interwoven, came instead into my father's possession and lined the high shelves of the Tomb Room at Watlington.

Chapter two

A DOUBLE LIFE

THE HOUSE STOOD on one of the bastions (as my father grandly called them) of the Chiltern escarpment. But only those who stayed in it were aware of this. Girdled by beechwoods, its brackeny park ran dead flat eastwards away from the view, clumped with monumental limes under which dots of rabbits changed places in the floodlight of the western sun. Only through a gap cut through the woods to the north-west could you just make out Magdalen Tower, using binoculars, from the drawing-room window.

A deer park had been enclosed here in the seventeenth century by the Stonors, an ancient local Catholic family, and they had built a small house in it, perhaps as a sort of shooting lodge and escape from the rigours of their draughty E-shaped house in a combe on the way to Henley. But they sold it in 1758 to a retired colonel, who built himself a sensible, unpretentious red-brick Georgian box facing it across a courtyard. Victorian and Edwardian successors had inserted unconvincing wings to link the two and turned the shell of Stonor's building into domestic offices. The south wing of 1910 had been the work of the lady from whom my parents bought the place in 1921 — "fiery-faced Freda" to them, but attractive enough, it seems, to have been the mistress of Kitchener, whose room still bore his name.

The place had been preferred to other South Oxon competitors because it was "on chalk" and 750 feet above sea level, which was then thought to be healthy, though in the dank mists that enveloped it in winter we often doubted this. Aesthetically they thought it left a lot to be desired. The Victorians had stuffed the garden with conifers and island beds, muffled Col. Tilson's brickwork in creepers, substituted plate glass for his Georgian sashes and papered his symmetrical hall with a black and gold flock said to have been chosen from the Great Exhibition. My parents set about re-Georgianizing it with enthusiasm (it was "their" period), replacing glazing bars, importing chimney-pieces and panelling and hiring a fashionable architect, Philip Tilden, to paint in the hall a rather cold classical *trompe l'oeil*. The garden took longer — indeed a thickset corduroyed labourer, described to us affectionately by my father as "Martin, my slave", sweated for years removing overgrown spruces, grubbing up laurel shrubberies and digging ha-has. In due course symmetrical yew hedges enclosed a formal frontispiece marked by Tilden's urns on red brick piers and an Italian Romanesque column as central feature.

As schoolchildren we were perpetually coming and going, and every time we came home "come and see the Improvements" would be the cry. This was a first taste of architecture, of the smell of building materials, and conferred on me a delight in any new thing, which I have never lost, partly because my maternal parsimony never allowed me to over-indulge it. Eventually my parents were induced by Lord Gerald Wellesley, who had the gift, useful in an architect, of making fun of the inadequacies of people's houses without necessarily hurting their feelings, to symmetricalize the Victorian north wing in a boring manner out of scale with the house. This produced a brand-new guest-suite which they painted peach colour, with pickled pine furniture, chintz-skirted dressing-table and Lalique lamps — very modern. The bathroom they lined with imitation pink marble they charitably bought from Gerry Villiers, another friend, who sold the stuff. But Gerry Wellesley fortunately failed in his bid to give the south side the same treatment.

Both Gerrys, ex-diplomats, were hard-up at the time, but had nothing else in common. Wellesley enjoyed what Meredith called an "indignant contentment", but his prospective ducal grandeur and touchiness were redeemed by a mischievous wit, often considered too *risqué* for us. Villiers, a large, athletic man, played golf with my father at Huntercombe and was often invited for the rabbit slaughter in the park, in which the wretched creatures were driven from bracken patch to patch, offering a quick shot in each narrow ride, and might survive a dozen dashes before succumbing. He had an emphatic, even explosive manner, concealing unease. My father offered what patronage he could. The 1920s abounded in ex-officers "down on their luck", and his correspondence contained countless begging letters, relying on dead friendships, of an abject kind seldom seen today. He responded with unfailing generosity.

He kept every letter he received, however trivial, binding up men and women in separate red volumes that eventually filled a whole wall of the Tomb Room. The reader can skip the next few paragraphs in

which I record some of the writers, *habitués* of Watlington, as a
recognition of his industry as well as their strong individualities.
There were, for a start, my mother's "girl friends", most of them
named Helen or Gladys. Unclubbable by nature, and too impatient
for committee work, my mother was nevertheless, like most of her
compatriots married to Englishmen, dependent in her early years here
on this circle of intelligent young American women, who spent hours
exchanging letters. The thickest volume, spanning twenty years, is
from Gladdy Huntington, a wildly funny, desperately sensitive
romantic, who made fun of her rather solemn husband Constant, a
high-minded publisher from her home town. A novelist or play-
wright *manquée*, she saw herself as a passionate Jamesian heroine, in
love with Europe, with the Renaissance, with Italy (less so with
England and its climate: she was apt to be depressed in their house in
Sussex). The racialist trial and execution of Sacco and Vanzetti in
America were a torture to her. She even wept at our dim Sunday
service at Christmas Common because Rev. Cox was so unbelievably
old and decayed: she wept a lot. Her friend Mildred Gosford was the
opposite — a reserved, rather grand Bostonian (a Carter) divorced
from an Irish peer and living a good deal in France, but deeply
attracted to my mother, whose outwardly radiant family circumstances she envied wholly without rancour. The prettiest of the
American women was Eleonora Day, for whose sake my father put up
with her notoriously boring US army colonel (who ranked the male
sex in order of merit as "a fine chap", "a chap", "a hairy-heeled chap"
and "not a chap at all"). Most of these women friends, whose wilful
and independent natures had led to difficult or broken marriages,
came to stay on their own. To us the most glamorous was English —
the beautiful, hard-up, farouche Ruby Lindsay, with her shock of dark
hair, a brilliant fellow-joker with my father. But I was also much
taken by *her* opposite, Horatia Seymour, a pale, fastidious lady,
dogged by ill-health and poverty, the victim, we thought, of some
disastrous love affair, whose cool, ironical intelligence I found easier
to cope with.

On the whole the women who came to Watlington were stronger
personalities than the men. To my mother the reason was obvious.
My father preferred women, and they fell for him, she knew, more
than men for her. She was always conscious that his end of the table
was where the fun was, and that attentiveness to her was distracted,

not least by his enjoyment of an audience. She accepted this with a fine equanimity, partly because she loved his jokes herself. Of course, "lions" did come, most of them first met in London, after they moved from Belgravia into a larger but, we thought, much more commonplace house in Hill Street (neatly excised in the blitz and still a yawning gap). They were mostly literary or artistic — Clive Bell, Eddie Marsh, Shane Leslie, Geoffrey Scott, Ned Lutyens, Boris Anrep, the Granville-Barkers, the Harry Grahams, Margot and Puffin Asquith. But my father remained faithful also to quiet, obscure men of whom Bear Warre, an unsuccessful architect, was our favourite — the splendidly good-looking, gentle son of a formidable headmaster of Eton.

Conversation round the long mahogany table was, whenever possible, general — not yet a lost art in England. This enabled the stars to shine but was intimidating for the young, whom my father would often call upon for an opinion. Before 1930 the talk tended to be about how to live, on the lines so irresistibly established by E. M. Forster and Virginia Woolf. Thereafter it inevitably turned political in a manner that professional politicians would have thought more frivolous than it was. The stereotype of the naughty twenties and the serious thirties found no reflection at Watlington.

The first man in the visitors' book in 1921, and the last in 1943, was Desmond MacCarthy. He and my parents had become friends in the early days of the war through a chance meeting between my mother and his — a tiny, hugely affectionate widow, German-French, who lived to a great age in a gloomy mansion flat off the Edgware Road. All three suffering, as such people do in wartime, from intellectual and social starvation, they became immediately intimate. I write "three" because his wife Molly, a sensitive writer herself, of whom they were all fond, seldom accompanied him on account of shyness and increasing deafness: she could not cope with the high style of talk in the big dining-room at Watlington. Indeed that gale of talk heard through a closed door which one had to open and confront intimidated us all. To Desmond, of course, it was the breath of life. We now think of the years between the wars as the last great age of talk in England, before the onset of mumbling and the service chores of hosts and hostesses killed it. (This may be no more than the old myth of the Golden Age, so infinitely regressive. Thus George Lyttelton writes of the Edwardian, "we didn't in the least realize at the time it was a Golden Age: in fact I am pretty sure the real Golden Age was before the Boer War".) Certainly to Desmond the great age of talk had ended with Oscar Wilde. "People are so haunted by the fear of being bored — or of becoming bores themselves, which is worse — that the talk flitters about too restlessly. . . . What people seem to want from you is a neat little pellet of an opinion which can be flipped across a table. . . . But I like the company of people who go hacking on at the same subject, even if that is only how to get a lawn in good order." He wrote this in the way he talked, catching a momentary truth, a side of the truth, and relishing it with a long chuckling yes, yes, yes, while his mind moved on. He even pretended to some nostalgia for the grand manner. "The only talker I have heard who in conversation will launch the high poetic phrase is Yeats. He will say that 'the music of Heaven is full of the clashing of swords' without seeming conscious that others might conclude that he was talking for effect. I like that myself. When I meet remarkable people whose company is coveted, I often wish that they would show off a little more."

He was in and out of the house a great deal, most of all in the four years each side of 1920, during which my father financed *Life & Letters* and set him up as its editor in a small room at the back end of Hill Street. Desperate pencilled messages on the hall table bore witness to his losing battle to be in time with things. These were the bibliophile years of the build-up of the Watlington collection of first editions, which threatened to explode the house until it was sold up after the war for exactly (we were told) what it had cost to buy. The epicene and sinister A. J. A. Symonds was a constant correspondent in his beautiful script, and Desmond himself contributed occasional additions. But to us schoolchildren the fat parcels of faded cloth bindings in every post had no glamour at all. To us Desmond represented above all the complexity and elusiveness of the truth. Systematic thinking learnt at school and semantic accuracy insisted upon by my mother were, I now realized, only explorer's tools, means to an unimaginable end. We were embarked, he made us feel, on a worthwhile expedition, even though, as he wrote: "Brilliance in youth is only almond-blossom and gives no promise of fruition. But how lovely, how amazing almond blossom is!" He liked young people, was curious about their intentions, dropped books on them which might help. In his sixties he said that he still thought of himself as a young man of promise.

But that was later. In our schoolroom years at Watlington none of these brilliant talkers took much notice of us as we sat at the children's table in the long, north-facing dining-room in the dull company of Mim or Frauly. Dullness was restful. "I love dull books," my father would say, and I was and remain in sympathy with Noel Blakiston's announcement on some country Sunday (according to Molly Mac-Carthy): "I think I'll walk by myself: it's duller." Governesses, being foreign, tended to be victimized, unlike the English staff, with whom relations varied between awe and complicity. They were symmetric-ally deployed — three in the kitchen, three in the pantry, three in the house, three in the nursery, three in the yard. There was no trifling with Mrs Taplin the cook, nor with Rosa the head housemaid, but Allen the butler was a slightly Malvolian figure, orotund and pompous on duty, but a jaunty figure out for a walk, and jolly in his tall, sunless, scrubbed deal pantry. And at the lower levels there was a lot of fun to be had teasing Waspy, the crinkle-haired footman so named because of his striped waistcoat, and Fishy, the sweet, slim, rather anxious second housemaid. Aside from these little hierarchies was Edith, my mother's maid and exact contemporary, a tiny Cockney sparrow of huge resilience and marvellous wit, who was to watch over my mother's horrific deathbed and survive her by sixteen years. She had a subtle role to play as recipient of brickbats and confidences from my mother, fellow-joker with my father and honorary member of my sisters' regular indignation meetings at the way they were all treated. My own dealings were mainly with the yard staff — with Wright, stolidly at the wheel of the capacious Rolls Royce (with me, whenever I was allowed, "on the box" beside him), in which we travelled across central Europe: he had the irritating tendency to drive too slow until admonished down the speaking tube, when he would accelerate to manic speed; and with Dimsdale, his appropriately dim side-kick, who helped me build my tree-house at the end of the park. With these two I endlessly discussed my main interest — cars and the heroics of Sir Henry Segrave and Sir Malcolm Campbell — which my parents did not share. I avoided the third in the yard trio, the sinister mechanic and epileptic Bird, who oiled the magnificent green and brass engine with great flywheel and slapping belt that generated our electricity and the clanking pump that extracted hard water from the chalk 500 feet below us.

Dimsdale's assistance indicated that the tree-house was a govern-ment-sponsored project; that is to say, one of my mother's bright ideas, perhaps drawn from some book, for filling up the long summer holidays. Another was a house in a fox-hole she had noticed in Dean's Wood. Summoning a couple of sisters, members of a club they were privileged to belong to called The Obedient Band, I dutifully collaborated as always though this time I found the wrong hole, a wide shallow depression where we struggled fruitlessly to push lengths of beech into its stony ground, consequently to be reprimanded and reduced to tears. The haunts I really cared for did not have to be built at all. We were all pantheists. Elves of hills, brooks, standing lakes and groves were real to us. Individual trees had good and bad characters, obscure corners of the garden, deep in bushes, betrayed like palaeolithic sites by the remains of ritual meals that we had squatted there. There were passages in the house where it was impossible after dark to look over one's shoulder, statues in the garden that came and went in the moonlight. Snakes and rats watched us from under barns, hedgehogs and baby rabbits were briefly adopted and soon buried. We looked through our legs at wolves and sunsets, or with one eye open at worm's eye level gazed up at the great bridges and towers I had built, and at my great clockwork battleship, as she ploughed her way through the duckweed to the great harbour I had created in the pond in the park. Lurking thus, impenetrably concealed, she represented me.

But solitary dreamer and vagrant I could not for ever be. My 1925 diary gives an impression of assiduous activity:

M. Bussy finished my picture at 11 and I showed it to Mummy who thought it very good. Then she went to Henley in the Lagonda. My golf lesson was put off because Bird and Dimsdale had got gassed when mending the ice-machine. So Daddy and I played 4 sets of tennis — 6–1, 6–0, 6–0, 6–1 to him. Then we went and shot a partridge. It rained all afternoon. We painted, played indoor cricket, rode our bikes indoors. After tea I went on with my drawing of the house, then we played "Pass". Daddy read *Catriona* after supper.

The summer jungle that surrounded and tantalized us was, one now forgets, only accessible in dry weather. Most of the time, we were stuck in the house, which had its own mysteries and potentialities. Its piecemeal building had left it with lots of little winding staircases and changes of level, complicated attic passages and what my father called frogholes, where hideouts could be established, preferably too low for grown-ups to stand up in. At dusk all this became spooky, and the moment of having to leave the panelled library, with its parchment shades and its walnut radiogram belting out Brahms, and go up into the creaky darkness, while a relief from reading one's approved book, was also a test of courage. Up top, when one got there, was another plainer, more relaxed circle of light and warmth, manned by an ironing nursemaid or sleepy governess. Here one could procrastinate indefinitely, before facing the ice-cold of one's unheated attic bedroom. Mine had a bull's eye window in the front pediment, on the central axis of the whole place, instilling Renaissance principles on which I was later to plant a lime avenue. But it was the house's Victorian ramifications much more than its Georgian symmetries that appealed to us. The Game, a sort of hide-and-seek invented by me to exploit them, was an exhilarating, exhausting exercise for children's parties, always won by the home team and still played, in reduced circumstances, by a third generation.

My room, of course, was a fortress. It had two frogholes of its own behind the panelling, where I was always liable to be. Sets of Scott, Henty, Stevenson and Conan Doyle lined the walls, with the eight volumes of Arthur Mee's *Children's Encyclopaedia* (all of which I read) and my three favourite history books — *Our Island Story*, Van Loon's *Story of Mankind* and (later) the Quennells' *History of Everyday Things in England*, inscribed by grandpa Esher in 1921 "a foretaste of *real* history" — a judgement which his own career consistently belied. When not reading, I found H. G. Wells's *Floor Games* (which were designed to exploit the hills and dales of eiderdowns) highly suggestive, and most of all his advocacy of Lot's Bricks. These smooth cement blocks, black and creamy-white in a variety of shapes and sizes, produced chunky, highly abstract architecture not unlike what W. M. Dudok and F. L. Wright were doing at the time.

It is often true that solitude is self-indulgent; but not, perhaps, in a boy of eight, when it is generally self-protective. Whatever its merits, prep school tore the cloak away. This, my first prison, was tucked away in North Oxford — a hotchpotch of bleak, yellow-brick, newish (c. 1900) buildings backing on to the Cherwell, in which a portly PT instructor, ex-army, taught us little shrimps to swim, standing waist-deep in the muddy water. Rooks, unknown at Watlington, cawed melancholy in the elms. Summer was not too bad, with cricket to watch and fun in the hay and plots where packets of seeds could be sown, though the long daylight allowed appalling things to happen out of sight. In the ha-ha below the headmaster's croquet lawn a Dutch boy had all his hair pulled out, and in the outdoor latrines, where we sat in long rows after breakfast, a gang beat up my best friend before my eyes. Cold baths for all began the day, and in winter, in the noisy common room with pitch-pine roof, we clustered on the radiators, our fingers bandaged for chilblains. The passages smelt of sweat and mutton, which we chewed in the yellow-brick dining-hall under the Honours Boards recording scholarships to the public schools. In the yellow-brick chapel I prayed that I might win one.

When not horrific, the place was absurd. In the gym, before admiring mothers with shingled hair, we danced slow waltzes or foxtrots with one another, wearing football stockings, knicker-bockers and white gloves. One mother brought down Monsieur Coué to lecture, and thereafter, to supplement my prayers, I would silently intone in my dormitory bed, "Every day and in every way I am getting better and better."

Absurdest was the teaching. My parents presumably chose the school for its special capacity to win scholarships to Eton, which they saw in purely honorific terms. Both were anxious that I should — my mother from American ambition ("work hard — play hard — that's the way to be a good schoolboy"), my father to atone for his own hedonistic schooldays. The method was mechanical and mnemonic. *Ammis, axis, caulis, collis . . . a, ab, absque, coram, de*, we endlessly intoned. History was taught by an elaborate wall cartoon for each period, taken in no particular order, in which, for example, a dachshund balancing a vase on its nose represented an obscure Norse chieftain called Olaf Trygvason (O laugh! Trick-vase on). Good fun, in its way. But to be good at such senseless learning must have brought an impoverishment of the imagination. Fortunate in after life were those boys who in instinctive protection switched off. Inatten-tion brought a bamboo cane on the hand, which hurt less if the thumb was pressed back. One master, said to be suffering from incurable shell-shock, flew into unpredictable rages but was only allowed to hit us on the head with a pencil. There were one or two women, chosen for their ugliness, including one who, musical though I was, put me off the piano. But, as often happens, the English master was the blessed exception — a soft Irish romantic novelist and poet called L. A. G. Strong, with an infectious passion for the music of words.

If I learnt this music, I did not use it for my letters home. These were as uninformative as I could make them, for I was determined, like many small boarders, to keep my two lives apart. At that age, one can only cope with one at a time. Their main note was anxiety and competitiveness. "I wish I could write you such nice letters as you write me, but everything goes on the same each day. Enthoven went to the dentist in London yesterday and I think it was the nicest day I've had for a long time. . . ." ". . . I've been moved into Upper Third and I've got awful people to beat this term. . . ." ". . . I will try and be more careful and accurate in future, although I hardly think I can try much harder than I have lately." My mother's were anxious too: had I worn my plate, taken my Beemax, made friends with the sons of her friends? I assured her I had, using Christian names for her benefit, though we never used them ourselves. In fact I seldom had. The boy I liked, called Rigg, obviously had the kind of parents mine dreaded. "I am so glad," I wrote in 1926, "the Strike is over. Of course everyone here is Conservative. Mr Williams wants to give the miners etc the 'cat'. Rigg's father wants to get out a machine gun. In fact there is only one other Liberal in the School." This was probably unfair to Mr Williams, though not, I dare say, to fascist Mr Rigg. The school's ethos, and the boys', was Tory only in the most old-fashioned sense. It was not the thing to be rich, nor to be in business at all. The best father to have was a down-at-heel Scottish laird, of an ancient, ruined family. Few could play the part, and certainly not mine, though as a boy he had, in a sense, been taught it. Determined not to fuss ("I am a warning to you children, not an example"), he left the bringing-up business to my mother, whose letters consequently were apt to be admonitory: "O you silly, silly little boy — why will you worry your mother so? It was very wrong of you and Mim not to take a jersey when you knew I wanted you to. . . . I've had a miserable week over it and I hope you're a little bit sorry." I came to dread them. His letters, by contrast, were innocuous and newsy, about dogs, rabbits, Watlington improvements and other things he thought would interest me: he steered clear of anything unpleasant.

Having started, as was to be expected, good at French and good at English, in the end I adjusted to the rest of the nonsense and became good at everything needed to do well in exams. This still bore the same relationship to real knowledge as chess to real life. In our last year we were cosseted like cerebral athletes. In perfect training, the scholarship squad of five, with the headmaster in charge, stayed in the White Hart in Windsor, travelling by taxi in and out of Eton. Between papers, in a strange limbo like casualties or ordinands, we sat on a bench in the playing fields, spirits sinking as the post-mortem proceeded. The results were posted up in the window of the school bookshop. Heart thumping, I went there with my parents. I was top of the twelve-year-olds, which meant that if I survived I would in due course be head of the school. Overjoyed themselves, they were astonished at how little emotion I showed, forgetting I suppose that one of the lessons I had already learnt was Kipling's attitude to triumph and disaster. Or else some instinct told me that the best was not yet to be.

Memory hoards the best and the worst, and its image of the sensitive ten-year-old, free to roam from field to field through eternal Augusts, then trapped in desolate dormitories through eternal Februarys, is one of the clichés of English middle-class autobiography. All education rubs in what we learned in our nurseries — that pride comes before a fall. The first snake you land on drops you from the Lilliputian dignity of prep school prefect into Long Chamber at Eton, a fifteenth-century barrack in which the tiny scholar spent his first year. Its curtained cubicles each contained a desk, bed and chair, a cold tap and a length of rubber tubing for filling a tin bath. This so-called "syphon" was used for beatings by the Captain of Chamber, a "trusty" granted this privilege by the sixth-form "swells" who ruled the establishment. Clubbable "scugs" socialized round the single fireplace in the centre of the huge high room; others pored over school books in their "stalls", until frozen out they joined the fireside circle where, as in any medieval hall, the companionships and cruelties of life were concentrated. Older boys assembled there on occasion to demand solo songs by breaking voices, to time a high-level race across the chimney-breast, to test knowledge of school colours and customs. Failure or peccadilloes meant nine strokes with the syphon. At intervals a distant cry of "Here!" sent us all clattering along passages and up or down uncarpeted stairs, the last arrival to be despatched on some shopping or other errand. My own fagmaster, perhaps without *arrière pensée*, offered me the refuge of his room, which I was too shy to accept, but did not hesitate to beat me on occasion. For the first year or

two tiny Collegers, conspicuous in their voluminous gowns, found
themselves in classes with oafish slow developers twice their size, who
had helped them on their way by random kicks in Fourth Form
Passage. The Master in College, a hirsute, fidgety misogynist,
referred to such hostile elements as "undesirable Oppidans", a
description which only reinforced our priggish rejection of the
ordinary world. He had a frightening, bedtime habit of creeping about
the passages in gym-shoes, so that he could fling open one's door and
catch one doing whatever one was. Or suddenly "Brett . . .
Brett . . . Brett . . . wanted" would echo down the worn deal
passages, in the soft half-hour before bedtime, and one must toughen
up, put on one's gown, and appear before the twelve members of the
sixth form, sitting at ease in their supper room. It might be a single
beating, or a mass one of a whole year which was thought to be above
itself. Fear and anxiety were among our earliest lessons, and it could
take a lifetime to unlearn them. But heroes did protest, among them
A. J. Ayer, whose courage I admired ever after.

And so through all winters and weathers we breathed the actual
English air and kept warm by effort, by singing, by unhunching thin
bodies and running the breath out of them. This brought its own
reward, when ragged and floppy from the football field, like a climber
at last off the mountain, we shuffled home through thickening dusk
and into steaming baths, which we straddled four abreast, barking and
howling. Later, scrubbed and shiny, we would sing in rough Latin at
Prayers and in smooth English at "Secular Singing", in prissy,
hermaphrodite English, expurgated ballads beloved of schoolmasters.

College was an oligarchy whose atmosphere changed with the
personalities of the ruling few. But unlike the Oppidan world outside,
where bum and crook and saint and snob were absorbed into a much
larger and looser society, the tone was set by the background of most
of us — the Professions, the Church, the Civil Service — and retained
a certain stuffiness whether hearties or aesthetes happened at a given
moment to be in charge. The typical extremes were the plodders,
conservative, conscientious, sweating it out in the morasses of the
Wall Game, splashing doggedly through icy watercourses, coming in
third in every exam and safe home at last to a scholarship at King's,
and the eccentrics, left-wing, wayward, laughable at games, who
corresponded with the Kaiser, evaded or outwitted authority, and
either won the race or forgot it was on. Too clever by half, surviving

in a hostile world by verbal dexterity, they seemed priggish and arrogant until an environment of their own choosing enabled them to drop their guard. The standard of living for the 50 or so unprivileged Collegers depended largely on which type happened to predominate at the top. With a government of the Right, life was severe and Arnoldian and fear stalked the corridors. With the Left in power, amnesty and gaiety alternated with unpredictable gusts of impatience. Successive Captains of the School recorded in a secret book kept for the purpose these changes in the political climate, with their own modest efforts at reform or reaction. Real change, needless to say, was imperceptible.

Meanwhile the great mass of the school carried on with its continuous performance as microcosm of English life. Most worked precisely as hard as they judged necessary to reach their personal standard of achievement, and played games fitfully (the fits when being watched). Dedicated minorities drove themselves to their moral or physical limits. Some prayed hard and lived upright lives. Some developed amazing techniques of sponging and evasion. Some smoked, some gambled. Some oscillated nervously between different influences; others pursued with myopic concentration a private dream, building a racing car or playing bagpipes in the School of Mechanics, which was the only building remote enough to be licensed for the purpose.

Unlike a prep school, always somewhat beleaguered in its Victorian mansion by the outer world of corner shops and "oiks", thickets and Odeons, Eton, like some great medieval monastery, was a world of its own, with its own long High Street as obsequiously ancillary as any estate village, and overlooked from Wyattville's battlements by the Monarchy itself, which had set up those 70 poor scholars with their Master, Precentor and choristers in their enormous Perpendicular chapel, as showy a demonstration as Chambord that when the King copied a new idea he could out-build any subject. We 70 were daily reminded by Latin incantation that we were the original Eton, but in reality we were only courtesy Etonians, wholly lacking, indeed encouraged to repress, the frivolity and self-assurance that were the school's strength and weakness.

It was not a particularly exalted period in the history of the place. "Down he plunges, King of waters, foaming over Boveny Weir!" my father would sing in his bath. This seemed to me a rather inflated description of the quiet and oozy Thames, down to which we would wander, through lanes lost in cow parsley, for raucous swims. Our space–time scale was different, and by it none of the prizes or beauties or dreams of Eton life looked so big. Nobody any longer chaired the winners of School Pulling or knew who was on the Select of the Newcastle. We thought the idealization of school life, the grandeur of the great, the adulation of the small, the inflated sense of the importance of the whole episode, childish when it was not repellent, and by the time we reached our last summer, once described by William Cory as "the pearl in the crown of years", we were looking forward and not back. We were probably lucky not to experience the sensualism and narcissism of Cory's Eton, whose influence on the last two generations had been blown to bits by the war, to be succeeded by the brittle cynicism of the smart twenties. Guy Burgess, then a sour cartoonist, had a drawing in some ephemeral magazine of a disgusting old father, drunk, toothless, hat bashed in after some fight on the Mound at Lord's and his epicene and elegantly *insouciant* son, dead bored by the whole thing — a half-truth in fact, since we still cared passionately about the Eton and Harrow match, whose glamour, as we got older, was enhanced by assignations with our marvellously dressed girl friends, who were almost indistinguishable from the champagne and strawberries.

We arrived in the year of the General Strike and left in the second year of the Great Depression, but nobody saw such events as any sort of threat to the place. Revolutionary personalities like Mahatma Gandhi and Ben Tillett, the Trade Union militant, addressed the Political Society in an atmosphere of amused, almost affectionate, irony — such was the euphoria, or bravado. In our microcosm, where all the follies and vices of mankind were adumbrated, an easy-going tolerance prevailed. Too often this disguised a lazy refusal or inability to cope with other people's seriousness, and at its worst it could degenerate into boorish cynicism and arrogance. In the High Street tailors and hosiers you could still see the old order in full flower. The manner with tradesmen varied between the familiarity which centuries of servility had taught them to respond to and the arrogance which sent them into their shells. To us shocked observers from the middle levels it never occurred that these "swells", sampling a new kind of chocolate like gourmets, ordering made-to-measure shoes, were only greedy schoolboys, eventually to be matured, as in the past, by some foreign war. A local by-election was grasped as the perfect opportunity to demonstrate our equal contempt for politicians of all parties. This was all very fine and life-enhancing, but it was risky in the world we were growing up in, and on the whole it did not pay off. People and parties are not, for one thing, equal, and their differences are more deeply based and need more imagination to handle than we were warned. Of my friends, those who were not killed in the war and were not absorbed by more or less hereditary occupations had to dismantle and reassemble themselves, or else found themselves hard to sell in the world of the mid-century. Too few Etonians could face the grind of the professions or of the Civil Service, where their courage and unorthodoxy would have cheered everybody up. Too many were content with traditional life in the City, the Army or Conservative politics, where they could count on grammar school boys to do the remembering. Even in College work, though done, must not be seen to be done, and in the rest of the school only an insignificant minority ever got the hang of it.

Storms in our College teacup did not ruffle the surface of the great School itself, whose diversity, continuity and manifest superiority we took for granted. Among the symbols of this was the extraordinary longevity of the staff at all levels. I was greeted by middle-aged clerks and tradesmen who had been middle-aged in my father's time, and long-retired Victorian housemasters shuffled daily into Chapel, one of them a broad, bent old man called Broadbent. Another, Toddy Vaughan, even older, gave large lunch parties at which I got drunk on cider. Those still in harness, generally known by some neat nickname, were well aware of popular opinion of them and for some it must have been hard to take. Lazy eccentrics could buy approval on the cheap; serious teachers had to be outstanding to earn it. Ultimate symbols of continuity were, of course, the Provost, M. R. James, a rubicund and distinguished bachelor whose Shakespeare Society it was an honour to belong to, and the Headmaster, the clever, handsome, histrionic C. A. Alington. So long as these tutelary deities sat on their carved Victorian thrones all was well with the world, if by no means with our half-formed adolescent personalities.

My mother's inability to communicate love, my father's sensitive determination not to step too readily into her place, had left me short of it, with a need for friends. The egregious Rigg had been succeeded at prep school by Keith Thomson, a dapper, clever fellow, sophisticated for his age, with the important advantage at that stage of life of a beautiful elder sister. We stuck together for a year or two at Eton and had a striped tie made to our design in the High Street, of which we were the only wearers. We were both slightly fancy fish out of water in the subfusc College atmosphere. But my instinct to conceal this was repeatedly thwarted by my parents. I could not prevent my mother *telephoning* mother-hating Marsden (Master in College in my early years) and fussing about trivialities, and they did not hesitate to drive into Weston's Yard in a new 40/50 Rolls Royce, out of which he stepped wearing (horrors!) an overcoat with an astrakhan collar. But by the time I was fifteen I had other preoccupations, having acquired my first girl friend, Anne Vesey, a blonde, blue-eyed, precocious schoolgirl of whom my sister Jinny properly disapproved. Her letters, infinitely more fun than Anne's, were breezy and affectionate, remaining so even when she and Rosemary Peto entered a passionately political phase at thirteen. ARE YOU A LIBERAL? she demanded to know in three successive letters. "*Answer me!* . . . I went to the House of Commons on Tuesday with Rosemary. Awfully interesting debate. Committee stage of the Coal Mines Bill . . ." But I had other things on my mind. I wrote to my mother: "Please don't think I am sceptical of my preparation for Confirmation . . . I have always prayed frantically at the beginning of the half and before Trials, and even before cricket matches, that I might not funk catches and so on . . . when I forget or am too hurried to pray in the evening I feel a complete ass . . . it is such a dirty trick to neglect God when he has helped me so much." Though He never did much for my cricket, I had certainly begun to win every prize that was on offer.

In 1930, when I was sixteen, my grandfather Esher died, and with him a decade supposed to be so liberated, creative and full of fun, but for me the age of anxiety. It was the Devil's Decade to come that would be our age of escape, though as it wore on we would find we had the Furies at our heels. Meanwhile we grew up, and bliss was it in that dawn to be alive. I knew I had the gifts that in those days were supposed to guarantee success. But the bad fairy at my christening had brought two other presents — a compulsion to succeed and a longing to be liked — or, for those who prefer the stellar version, a typically Cancerian conflict between ambition and diffidence. No one at the party noticed her, least of all myself.

Chapter three

ALMOND BLOSSOM

A MOMENT ARRIVES when youth, isolated at first from parents by its sense of inadequacy, is isolated by the joy of youth itself, like a mist of tears through which one can hardly see the adult world. In 1932 my mother gave me a blank "commonplace book" into which I copied every passage, from *Romeo and Juliet* to *Richard Feverel*, that caught the dizziness of first love and the infinite potential of unfocused creativity. I wished to emulate Leonardo's famous advertisement of all the things he could do. In my last two years at Eton, the problem was to choose. Having shared the Rosebery Prize for history with Jo Grimond, I thought I must have made good my escape from the Mods-and-Greats treadmill, but classical tutors conducted a dogged rearguard action, and it was true I loved the idea of Greece and writing Greek verse. Then the Loder Prize (for public speaking) caught the eye of Tory talent-spotters, who set upon me when I was *ex-officio* invited to some dinner in the House of Commons. Or was it writing, which came much too easy and inevitably led to editing the *Chronicle* and various ephemeral magazines? Easiest of all came art: after the New College Scholarship, as a sort of licensed escapist, I could set up my easel on warm afternoons and paint the dusty *terre verte* of the June elms and the Monet-like intricacies of Luxmoore's Garden. At sixteen I had written firmly to my father: "I intend to devote as little time as I can to the school curriculum and attempt to absorb some real culture by reading." Shades of his own dilettantism! He resisted his inclination to object, provided I consulted some grown-up "guide" and always had "something really *difficult*" on hand — advice I have taken ever since.

But "real culture"? I used the word in the only sense it then had — Arnold's sense of "the best that has been thought and said in the world". But I did not mean it: if the advice I got suited my inclinations I took it, my inclinations, like any adolescent's, being towards romantic writing that celebrated the wonders and mysteries of the physical world. Cash from prizes I spent on Ruskin, Roger Fry and

Clive Bell, or on the Laureates Masefield and Bridges: I was particularly taken with *The Testament of Beauty*, a pedantic, affected work which my tutor admired and which I hoped met my father's requirement on difficulty. If not, Hardy's *Dynasts* certainly did. But it was Brooke, Sassoon and Graves with whom I really identified, and Belloc who implanted in me the prolific weed of Fine Writing. César Franck and Sibelius, which must have sounded terrible on my wind-up portable, were as far as I had got in music — heady stuff, suitable for seventeen, but worlds away from the spare, sardonic, insecure European culture within which we actually lived. To this culture, using the word now in its more modern sense, I could not hope to find any guide at Eton. The world emerging under the influence of Marx and Freud, Lawrence and Joyce, Picasso and Le Corbusier, Rilke and Kafka, was a closed book there. If the staff had any mechanism for discussing such matters, it might have been argued that boys must walk before they can run, and that the European culture of the 1930s had better be a university preoccupation. But probably it had no such mechanism, and I never met a master who mentioned such people.

The Europe we annually visited was a very different kettle of fish. In the Christmas holidays of 1926 my first Eton reports were poor and my father hauled me into his study, where I dissolved in tears. He promised a journey to Spain in the spring if I improved, which I immediately did. So Easter 1927 found me sketching on my camp-stool in grey flannel suit and Homburg hat, watched by incredulous urchin contemporaries, in dusty corners of Toledo and Granada. Next year the same foursome — for it included my cousin Bunnie Heckscher, passionate for culture, in whom my mother saw a replica of herself — visited the cities of Emilia. I became a pint-sized expert on the Gonzagas, on Federigo Montefeltro, on Sigismondo Malatesta. In 1929 it was a motor trip via the French cathedrals to the Rhineland and Bavaria: we discoursed on Balthasar Neumann and Fischer von Erlach, and my diary was full of careful sketches of the south transept of Beauvais and the onion spires of Donaueschingen, with learned chat about choir-stalls and clerestories. In 1930 it was Normandy, where we stayed with the celebrated ladies, Miss Sands and Miss Hudson, in their paper-thin transparent manor house near Dieppe, and then with Paul Maze, more splendid as man than as artist, and his large English family of Nelson girls, in a great watermill near Dreux. This was the other kind of culture, with other painters joining us for huge picnics in forest clearings. But the Grand Tour resumed in 1931. Easter we spent in 3, Foro Romano, Lord Berners' secluded house in the heart of Rome. This time a girl materialized, Jinny's friend Rosemary Peto, a spectacular blonde tomboy with whom I drove around in a carrozza, attracting a lot of welcome attention. Evenings I would walk to spaghetti suppers in her mother's lover's flat on the Lungo Tevere. Then through a soaking wet August we drove in easy stages across Europe to Salzburg: more architectural chit-chat, more sketches, then lots of Bruno Walter in the company of the smart and musical young — the future musical establishment of London. Here I never took my eyes off the pretty little soprano, Adele Kern — the first I had seen who looked like a human being. I suppose the last of the series, in the summer I left school, was a week with the famous Alice Keppel in her Villa Ombrellino overlooking Florence, with both the difficult daughters present in a large house-party where the talk was way above my head.

"Dear, dear Abroad", my father called it, and it must have been the fulfilment of their dream in the anxious months when he was courting her on Long Island and she finally, after breaking their engagement in panic, settled to marry him. They were both dedicated sightseers. She liked princely interiors and the birthplaces or deathplaces of her heroes — Goethe, Beethoven, Schubert. He was a tireless hunter for the Baroque, newly discovered by the Sitwells. But fortunately they were not too solemn about it. Painters like the Italians Taddi, Gaddi and Daddi and the Dutchmen Pot and Codde supplied comic relief. They could laugh at themselves when, having admired a fine fresco, they found that they had misread Baedeker and it was dated 1879. We were all art snobs. Munich's gallery of modern art was "the worst I have ever strayed into — literally nothing but German-Victorian, the worst Victorian of all", and a roomful of the Viennese *Secezzion*, entered by accident, "made Mum sick". She would stamp her foot at officials who denied her what she wanted, then humanly transfer her rage to me if I foolishly took their part. So there were dark days when, squeezed between them in the sick-making back of the Rolls, whose cavalry twill upholstery was impregnated with his tobacco smoke, I felt trapped in the line of fire. I suppose all this emotion, industry, note-taking, sketch-making, must have taught me, in its old-fashioned way, a lot of art-history and some discrimination, but I never associated it with my own art work or felt impelled by it to be an architect myself.

Another cold and wintry April, 1932, we were to take the Orient

Express for our last journey of the series, bound for Budapest and Vienna. "I sat on deck and watched the horizon appear and disappear above the railings, too depressed to read. It was very unwise of me to see Pom at the last moment: I should have known it would kill the first days of the trip." This was a new kind of heartache. But I rapidly recovered, particularly when Jinny joined us, brown and hearty from her *Töchterpensionat* on the Starnberger See and happily committed to the German youth cult, which seemed a harmless if slightly absurd craze. Budapest was grey and shoddy, the picture galleries unheated and deserted, and in the tea-rooms the heavily moustached tzigane violinist had only us to sidle up to ("he reminds me of somebody," says my father . . . "myself, I think"). Vienna put a brighter face on its poverty, but there was something forlorn about the widowed *Gräfin* toying with frugal lunches at Sacher's and the thinly attended Opera: a sense of distant political thunder. Staying too long, we scraped the sightseeing barrel in locked and silent Baroque palaces and twilit collections. How different was Munich! "We passed Hitler's headquarters, flying his huge Swastika flag, the garden full of earnest young men saluting each other gravely as they pass up and down, and *Deutschland Erwache!* carved boldly over the door." It was a joy to come home to the medal-ribboned stewards and red silk lampshades of the Dover boat-train.

Some time in that year I told my parents that I wanted to be an architect. Sensually, it was the fun of the eternal building operations at Watlington and the charm of Lutyens' presentation of the Great Game, sketching on his knee while I sat at his feet in the Morning Room. Intellectually, I believed I was too cerebral and too unimaginative to be an artist (I did not then realize that you can let the first lie fallow and cultivate the second), yet too wayward for public life. So this seemed the happy mean for me; but it was a blow for my parents. My mother, blissfully staying with the Granville-Barkers in Paris, wrote: "So Victor [Cazalet] failed to persuade you of the advantages of a public career? Don't think I mind you being an architect — I think it's a fine profession, only in England there's such an old tradition in favour of people of your sort 'serving their country' either in the Army or the Govt. or Civil Service, and *everyone* I meet who has heard about you just takes it for granted that you are cut out for public life, either in Diplomacy or the House of Commons. They all look a little dashed when I say, Oh no, he wants to be an architect." From now on "they" were to be dashed quite often.

And who was Pom? Pom Pike she was called — her father an Anglo-Irish soldier whose family had been settled in Co. Cork and Co. Wexford since the seventeenth century. Unlike his younger brother, Max, a high-spirited airman killed in the Flying Corps, and his much younger sister, the romantically beautiful and eccentric Rhoda Birley, he was a rather anxious, conscientious man, but he had the charm and distinction of a d'Artagnan, dressed with careless elegance and was above all (in Guards' parlance) "straight as a die". His wife, Olive Snell, intuitive, light-hearted, ambitious, was a fashionable portrait-painter, with what her friend Noël Coward called "a talent to amuse". She had "done" everybody from Greta Garbo to the Prince of Wales, my mother and us children included. In this January of 1932 she and my mother received invitations from a mutual friend, the dashing and attractive Lady Dashwood of West Wycombe, to send their eldest to a "young people's house-party". Both accepted, so off we separately went, dead scared, she from London, I from Watlington, she still at some Paris finishing-school, I still at Eton. Refugees from a noisy game of "Murder", I and this tall, dark, pale girl found ourselves alone in the dining-room. We had our first, earnest conversation. I was overwhelmed. A few days later, greatly daring, we had lunch at the Berkeley and I experienced for the first time the exhilaration of walking down a London street with a spectacular beauty in a great purple skirt (she was "in mourning" for some relative). I walked on air: joy, pride, anxiety, jealousy were to be the counterpoint of the coming summer.

The blaze of antique glory in which passed my last months at school was obviously bad for me. An arrogance appears for the first and last time in the leaving photographs I exchanged, as was the custom, with contemporaries. But my own desire was not to bask but to grow up, to escape into freedom and silence. The summer solstice at Watlington was a foretaste. Under a full moon, over the dewy turf, Pom and I walked on the rabbit-cropped Hill, car headlights flashing in the valley below, silent, certainly, and still shy of the potential of the occasion. August was our last *en famille*, as paying guests with the Oglanders at Nunwell in the Isle of Wight. Pom was across the water in their suburban villa on Hayling Island. At sunset I would climb Brading Down with binoculars hoping to catch some glimpse, and once I took the ferry and spent a night. But she had been left in charge of her small brother and was in a maddeningly maternal mood. I did not guess that she wore this (perhaps unconsciously) as a shield — that she was in love with a much more sophisticated admirer. To my long, neatly written, desperately insecure letters she replied in a hand as wild as an action painter's, friendly but fancy-free, as far as I could judge when I could read them.

Oxford fortunately offered every sort of distraction — at a price. Sending a cheque when she heard I was short, my mother wrote that she wished me to live the life of "a young man of position" — a Jane Austen phrase which I imagine only an American could use without irony. They had selected New College because they had been given to understand that a sensible and studious Wykehamist atmosphere prevailed there. But they would not have wished me too frowstily ensconced. For them, as for me, it was a matter of juggling rival attractions and commitments, keeping as many balls as possible in the air. Mere book-learning was the simplest, since exams came easy and I had no scholarly ambitions beyond them. The Modern History school was considered the soft option of every upper-crust *flâneur*, and I was not much taken with its New College tutors, Mr Wickham Legg and Mr Ogg. I consulted Desmond MacCarthy about philosophy, and he sent me a pile of books and a long and charmingly painstaking letter in which he put its case:

Philosophy does not make life happier or easier, but it makes it more interesting, and it may prevent one from taking too seriously things which let one down in the end. Thought adds to life the dignity if not necessarily the consolations of religion. It has been my saving.

But he correctly guessed it would not be mine. I was naïve enough to read a paper on aesthetics to the New College philosophers and to be humiliated by its easy demolition. Escaping the pipe-smoke into the frosty night and the canopy of stars (which you could see from a city in those days) I knew this was not my moral home. All the same I was too serious for the joky, flamboyantly un-Wykehamist Etonian minority on which one could so easily fall back. A letter from William Douglas-Home (quoting from one of my more soulful efforts in Speeches at Eton) gives my relationship with them.

Knowing, as I do, that you have felt impelled in the past to thrust game-cards upon me, muttering "look at those damn you! they're more in your line", while the out-pourings of Beethoven throbbed through my captivated brain — enough of that — I write to ask you to send me the card of that day I shot with you Nov. 8th — if you remember — with every expectation of receiving it by return of post. Now that the charms of — God, I feel sick . . . no . . . all right now — (as I say), now that the charms of shooting have me in thrall once more, the urge to bring my game book, that noble tome, up to date, is upon me. Thank you very much indeed. Note my note of crawling humility always employed with a purpose.

"The soul of Adonais like a star beacons from the———". They tell me that statue in Univ: may represent beauty, but *not* truth, because actually the chap was tasted by innumerable sharks.

I settled for History and was lucky to find two tutors in All Souls, E. L. Woodward and Richard Pares, who were perceptive enough to see through my own facility, help me to a comfortable congratulatory First, but deny me, quite rightly, their own Fellowship.

I found my friends, in the course of time, outside my College. Two lodging-houses in Beaumont Street held most of us. In No. 21 were two shy men of infinite good sense and lazy charm, Jo Grimond and Mark Pilkington, and two maniacs, Jasper Ridley and John Pope-Hennessey, the former a wayward, fantastical, fastidious creature, the latter (known to us as Botticelli) already a single-minded aesthete, reckless of common opinions. Up the road at No. 9 were Jeremy Hutchinson, Guy Branch, Micky Burn and the odd Greek or French friend, in Oxford for the fun of it. Here a more hedonistic spirit prevailed. It was Guy in particular, with his generous smile, his love and despair of life and his exquisite girl, the dancer Pearl Argyle, whom above all I envied and wished to emulate. And across the street, for a year he had contrived with great difficulty, lodged my cousin Maury Heckscher, who was hopelessly at sea, for all I could do, in this self-contained circle of elliptical, ironical people, who spoke a language so unlike his own. He fled to the far west of Ireland, where he felt far more at home by a turf fire among the peasants of Carraroe. Within a few years Maury was dead in an American army camp, Mark had been killed in East Africa, Guy lost with his Spitfire in the Battle of Britain, Jasper blown up in a minefield escaping out of Italy and Micky a prisoner at Colditz, having been captured at St Nazaire. It must always seem that the lesser among us survived.

I acquired in those years the sense, which stayed with me for good, that there was no time to lose. So I read like mad, and learnt languages, and painted pictures which I sold at Rymans in the High, and went to life classes at the Ruskin School, and worked at architecture, and gave parties, and chased up and down the London road at all hours of the night. We had a copy made of the key to a door in the wall at New College, which made it possible to enlarge our experience of life in a gentlemanly way. But gentlemanly it still was. We were under-graduates, not students, and our relations with girls tended to be romantic. They, for one thing, did not grow up or appear in public till they were seventeen or eighteen,★ and then stepped gingerly into the unknown. "Lionel dear (I have never been able to discover how endearing a term that is, but we'll risk it)." London dances (which we affected to despise) were beguiling because we knew that we were better company than the average young guardsman or city gent and that we had the added charm of having to vanish like Cinderella and drive riskily off into the summer night. Entranced by these sudden appear-ances and disappearances, to the irresistible music of "Blue Moon", or "Stormy Weather", or "Night and Day", to the simple strains of the Georgian poets, our hearts embarked on their journeys in the mood of Siegfried Sassoon's poem of that name:

> As I was walking in the gardens where
> Spring touched the glooms with green, stole over me
> A sense of wakening leaves that filled the air
> With boding of Elysian days to be.
>
> Cold was the music of the birds; and cold
> The sunlight, shadowless with misty gold:
> It seemed I stood with Youth on the calm verge
> Of some annunciation that should bring
> With flocks of silver angels, ultimate Spring
> Whence all that life had longed for might emerge.

★"Jinny," wrote my mother, "felt very much of a child compared with Rosemary, in a low-cut dress and with a beau. Certainly a gulf yawns between the 'out' and the 'not out'."

Cruel yet vulnerable, we inflicted and endured what seemed to us intolerable pain, and it was maddening to find old men like Logan Pearsall Smith writing smugly from under cover of the "safe, sad charm of those bogus heartbreaks".

It was all very well for that sheltered old aphorist, *habitué* of my parents' Hill Street dinner parties, to write in that cynical vein. It did not occur to me that he could ever have felt, for some boy, what I felt, sitting out a June sunset in a corner of the garden of the Trout Inn at Godstow, with Patricia Berry's letter in my pocket, ending our "affair". She was a slim, bosomy *gamine*, very correctly brought up by the old Camroses, and I had met her at our local Hunt Ball in the autumn of 1932. We hugged on dance floors, held hands in her parents' stuffy house in Seymour Place (later, like ours, taken out by a bomb) and I felt obliged, if I was to stay in the race, to load her with orchids. I loved her enough to stay with her parents in their plushy, ugly great house near Ascot, in a world which could never have been my own. It was as well, I suppose, since I have never been much good at shedding people, that in this as in other cases it was done for me. But the blow to pride, as well as the sudden deprivation, was that much harder. Other girls, tentatively or sentimentally or amusedly, had reassured my parents by providing "safety in numbers". But for a year and a half I had given my heart to her, and it ached horribly, for a few days.

Meanwhile Jinny and Nancy had been growing up too (black-haired Pinkie, with her fringe, still looked like a charming Japanese doll). Jinny, who should have gone to university (not done by girls in our circle), was "brought out" at a ball in a rented house in Curzon Street. Wearing a gold dress from Lanvin or Vionnet, poor Jinny was publicized by Francis Stonor, who did the catering, as the Golden Débutante, with the result that a small angry mob of unemployed gathered outside. This traumatic experience drove us all leftwards politically, and drove Jinny, after a hectic, rather drunken Season, out of Society altogether. Following her star, she became a German-style *Wandervogel*, determined to use my father's sense of fun and absurdity, which she alone inherited, as a weapon against everything they represented. Nancy, "the pretty one", was still "in the tunnel", their word for adolescence, which they treated like measles. There she perfected different weapons, more like my own — soft words and outer conformity — with which to confront the common enemy.

These tensions came to a head on a disastrous family holiday at Portofino. My mother had lately read a sentimental book by a German lady called *An Enchanted April*, and determined that she would rent, for that same month in 1934, the Castello of the story. There she found it impossible not to continue trying to improve us in various ways. Overlooking the toy pink and yellow port, we each sat in separate embrasures, writing furious diaries (or, in my case, drawing). Sisters flung out of meals, rushing up to bedrooms. Below, the pretty pale-grey cruisers and destroyers of the Mediterranean Fleet rode at anchor, dressed overall, and on mild evenings the Marines' dance music carried across the water. We could not enjoy any of it.

This was the Baldwin era, and you could still put personal relations ahead of politics. My hero among writers had declared that "if I had to choose between betraying my country and betraying my friend, I hope I would have the guts to betray my country". So I supported the Union resolution not to fight for it, explaining sententiously to my father that I would "fight" (whatever that meant) only for the Covenant of the League of Nations. I sent a letter (unpublished) to *The Times*, sickened by Baldwin's failure to use oil sanctions against the absurd Mussolini. Little fights like this, under international auspices, might with luck ward off the ultimate horror. The thought of arming for *that* filled us with despair, which we exorcized by frivolity. Communist acquaintances might heroically get themselves beaten up by Mosley's bodyguards. The rest of us, non-joiners, closed our minds to canvassers whether from Left or Right or from the more persistent Oxford Group, and opened them to narcissistic curiosity and concern for one another and for those few dons who shared our preoccupations. But nothing in those years was obsessive: everything was worth a try, every experience the first of its kind. In the constipated architecture and poor acoustics of Oxford Town Hall, for example, Rachmaninov came on the stage, his expression impenetrably remote and abstracted, then sat down, and from that massive, you would think peasant's, physique produced sounds as delicate as the movements of a butterfly.

To remain glued to Constitutional History this May [I wrote home], is more than is humanly possible. I'd rather get a third. On the other hand London seems to be definitely not worth while, and this last weekend in Oxford has been a succession of parties. There were about five sherry parties and the OUDS supper after the last night of the play, which went on till five. Yesterday I lunched with Roy Harrod, a serious don of Christ Church who collects round himself all the gayest and least serious people in London, in the midst of which he sat silent. On Friday Prof. Lindemann, whom I had barely met, asked me to lunch and I found him tête-à-tête. He dabbles in politics, and is trying to get the Prime Minister to do something about air defence. He is also a High Tory and Churchillian on India, so I was hard put to it, trumping up second-hand arguments. I was defeated all round, as he is one of those maddening people who say you can't talk about India till you've been there. Tomorrow I am giving a slightly alarming dinner for Betjeman and Kenneth Clark and the two cleverest dons I know, Bowra and Crossman. I hope they will entertain each other.

Like Guy, come the long summer, I felt it absolutely necessary to be alone. A "reading party", such as the Balliol one that foregathered in Sligger Urquhart's chalet in the Alps, was not for me. Europe was cheap, and one of the great joys of leaving school was to have the run of it. One would start by walking in on one's sisters or girl friends at their finishing schools run by the austere Mlles Ozanne in the Rue Crévaux or by the fearsome Mrs L'Estrange above Florence. One could never be sure whether one would be allowed to take them out to lunch or be constrained to take tea with them in their own salon, with a chaperone behind a screen. Then would come the first motor-trip, books flattening the back tyres of second-hand Hornet or Midget, toy cars that shook to pieces on French *pavé*. All Europe saw our breakdowns, voluble ones in dingy French suburbs, silent moonlit ones on Spanish passes, crashes at Paris cross-roads, engineless freewheelings down Swiss hairpins. We were the advance guard of the GB army, and nobody had our spares. Every familiar tourist spot was pristine new to us, and we were (or we felt we were) the first to reach Santiago and Almuñecar, the first to live in Aix and St Tropez, the first to sit up all the way from Constantinople. The rest of the world could go hang; Europe was home to us.

My first free summer I drove my absurd two-seater, with its six tiny cylinders, to Compiègne, then a sleepy, dim town beside its great château and royal forest, where I was to improve my French in Madame Coze's town house, backing on to an orchard — the dullest place imaginable. A handsome widow living with a spinster friend, she had two French-style doglets and the misfortune of a mongol daughter (whom I, ignorant of the disease, just thought rather ugly). One other decent Englishman completed the establishment, apart from the widow's lover at evening, and the boredom was blissful. Here I could recover from the teacup storms and stresses of the London Season, play its marvellous records, write long letters to girls: to Pom I wrote that all the little girls in Compiègne seemed to be called Christiane — her real name. Then I would take my paint-box into the remotest ride of the silent forest, the air laced with insects. On the Quatorze the rides echoed to a glorious parade of exotic cavalry — spahis, zouaves etc. — then the silence returned. At the end of August I drove the little car across Germany to Bayreuth, where I had a rendezvous with Jinny. My father, a tone-deaf but passionate Wagnerian (he identified with Wotan), had given us tickets for a solid week there, including the whole of the *Ring*. Then two friends, boy and girl, joined us for a ten-day hike in the Thuringian Forest near Weimar. A chaperone was, of course, obligatory, in the form of a large-boned Munich *Gräfin* known to the girl's mother. She did not add to the joy of life, but there was an infinity of it without her. In an inn visitors' book Jinny copied out the *Jugendmotiv* from *Rheingold*, with the words

> *Goldene Äpfel wachsen in ihrem Garten:*
> *Sie allein weiss die Äpfel zu pflegen.* *

Provincial France was depressed and shabby, the Riviera old-fashioned and beyond our means, Paris out of our depth. Spain was sinister and racked by dissension, Italy – romantic dreamland for our Forsterian parents – required cultural orthodoxy and homework. Greece was only visited by schoolmasters, Scandinavia by architects. But Munich and the Starnberger See, the pastures that rolled with their onion-spired churches to the feet of the Alps, Salzburg and the Tyrolean peaks and valleys through to Vienna — this was the territory of the young.

Hitler, who had taken power that year, was a figure of fun, cautiously referred to in conversation as "Mr Smith", and the swastikas drawn by small fingers in the dust on the car had no menace for us. "The Hitler craze is a bore," I wrote home, "but it doesn't seem to have spoilt this

---

*Golden apples grow in her garden;
Only she knows how to harvest them.

part of Germany. They enjoy dressing up and doing the Roman salute, and it gives young people something to do. They march about in companies singing marvellously: at Würzburg they woke us up singing at five."

The following summer, 1934, I was back, in a different foursome, with Nigel Fisher and Gloria Vaughan, who married soon after. The fourth was Pom. We had each come through a heartbreak of a different kind, and needed each other. I marked this moment by calling her by her real name, but in the Compiègne version, because without that "e" it sounded severe, even masculine. (Years later I found at Watlington a lock of hair that had belonged to a Christiana Brett in 1794 and settled permanently for that.) The obligatory chaperone this time was her Aunt Marjorie, who slept most of the way, shared out between the two cars. It was Oberammergau year, another uplifting and exhausting German ritual, after which they dropped me at the feet of the Alps and drove home.

Haus Hirth at Garmisch was an up-market, intellectual lodging house fashionable among the Salzburg set. Walter Hirth, a handsome, thickset, white-haired man, was content to play backup to his vivid, sunburnt, musical wife Johanna. In principle, everybody was "creative" — Katherine Cornell, the dramatic American actress, Robert Nichols, a melancholy English poet, the charming and musical Prince Ludwig of Hesse, a Dutch family party and some attendant girl aspirants, British or American. We were all supposed to be improving our German, but clever talk, which we could only manage in English, took priority.

All day, we scattered. In crystal air, I would stuff books into a rucksack, climb 4,000 feet in a couple of hours and read till sunset on the tip of some peak, looking down over ridge upon ridge against the dazzling light. The Zugspitze range and the Karwendel are the kind of mountains I have headed for ever since — climbable in a day, needing some route-finding, safe enough to be done alone, unsafe enough to have a spice of danger.★ What it is about mountains that glues my nose to train and plane windows I shall never know, nor why, looking up

★Sometimes this came from an unexpected quarter. Laughing, with friends, at a comically dressed clergyman we met on some mountain top, I leant casually against the tall wooden crucifix that marked the summit. The cross-piece immediately fell off and hit me on the head.

even at Cnicht, or Suilven, or Sgurr nan Gillean, I love the sense of having stood on that precise point against the sky. I only know that in me this lifelong passion dated from that summer.

The other bud of love was for C. We would give it a year, we had decided. But how could it not flower? As the months passed I knew my destiny stood before me, unmistakable, inescapable. I wished to escape, as usual. I was to share a London flat with Jo Grimond — the sensible next stage of life. Why must everything come to me so soon? In an essay at school I had made out that Keats's coupling of Beauty and Truth was a nonsense, but here they were, inseparable, in one person. I could not let her go. It happened to Jo; it happened to us all. Perhaps it was our instinct that we had no time to lose.

As our year moved to its emotional climax I felt the need at times for austerity and discomfort. "Absent thee from felicity awhile." I spent a freezing April reading and climbing alone in Snowdonia and a soaking week in the Lakes with Jinny. Come the summer and my *viva* at Oxford, it had become a matter of experience, no longer of vanity, that we were going to have somehow to reconcile marriage and architecture with a fellowship at All Souls, and we started house-hunting on Boar's Hill. But the College sensibly put an end to that nonsense: it must have been obvious that my heart was not in Oxford any more. And so, acting our parts as traditional bridal couples do, we were married in October at St Bartholomew's in the City by Dick Sheppard, whose pacifism, admired by us, was detested by the local incumbent (whose name, equally appropriately, was Savage). Remarkably for one so well grounded in travel logistics, it didn't occur to me that the reception was miles away in C's uncle Oswald Birley's studio in St John's Wood. A lot of the guests vanished into the traffic. In a dream, we drove off without our honeymoon luggage and had to go round the block and start again. After a couple of weeks beside the autumnal sea on deserted Hayling Island, we blithely sailed for Spain. This sounded a good idea: the sun would have left the rest of Europe; two years back, we had both fallen for the landscape, I in a clapped-out Renault with two Americans, C on a cruise with her parents, when she had been madly courted by a young Spanish aristocrat, sent packing as a "dago" by her father. Travelling on local trains and country buses down the impoverished east coast, we found the people grim and the itinerary exhausting. Something seemed wrong with the place: we had no idea that Franco was about to pounce. C finally fell ill in a fishing village on the south coast, while I sat in an empty hotel lounge above a pounding sea. A trio with an English fiddler (who was Laurie Lee) had only me to play to.

We were to join the Brett family at Haus Hirth for Christmas and some skiing. In fact in a prolonged thaw we sat in a row in the misty sunshine, reading the Russian classics. All three girls were now in simmering revolt. Jinny bore the brunt. She had had a rough time. Convinced she was the ugly duckling, overdressed in her Paris *trousseau*, oversold at her golden ball, she felt she knew no men, while Nancy was having the time of her life at Mrs Fyfe's fashionable school at Cambridge being taken out by beautiful undergraduates like Claude Phillimore and Donald MacLean. "Watlington," she wrote me, "will be peopled by your girl friends and Nancy's boy friends — slightly disheartening for a prospective deb." Nevertheless she had plunged gallantly into the fray, and when it was over had returned to Bavaria, her spiritual home and that of so many English girls of her kind, where she had spent most of the past year with the beloved Hoyos family in Munich. . . . Now she recklessly took on the parents single-handed, with moral but more circumspect support from the other two — Nancy in the afterglow of an autumn in Vienna, where with four friends (of the group described by Philip Toynbee as the Liberal Girls) she had shared the Bonham Carters' Swiss governess. This lady, whom they called Cuffy, later became a cult figure of the Oxford Fringe, where she set up house with her lover, Foxy Falk, and ran a much-loved haven of music and literature. Daughters of formidable mothers desperately needed this woman they could talk to. The circle of Cuffy Girls grew with the years, with Pinkie one of its most devoted members. But that winter she was still a tunnel-bound Cinderella — as my father called her. "She gets the Prince," he would say to cheer her up, but she did not believe it. They had wanted another boy, she well knew — indeed she had seen a telegram received at her birth from one of my mother's American cronies: "Are you sure? look again."

We often asked ourselves in later years why that war had to happen. The gorgon image of my mother, the rigorous disciplinarian, and the jolly image of my father, the frivolous dilettante, is unfair to them both. Both were latter-day romantics, high on symbolist poetry and the chivalric ideal. Their marriage was an escape together from worldly and distant (though so different) fathers and from shy, repressed mothers, she with this dark, sallow-faced, highly literate European (he did not look like, nor was he essentially, an English-man), he with an American straight out of Henry James, blue-eyed, outspoken, valiant for truth. But while he continued to enjoy the world and so learnt to manage it, she could not relax her will to improve it, or at least to improve us — a natural parental tendency, which can produce in children a lifelong, ineradicable habit of saying what people want, rather than the truth they need. It was unfortunate that we all inherited *his* sensibility (but only Jinny the sense of fun with which he protected it) and *her* uncompromising determination not to be pushed around. Over-sensitive and self-protective, we could not play the winning card of generosity that youth always holds in its hand. It was, after all, early days. We were still learners, while they, sociable and sought-after, were on top of the world.

That evening at Haus Hirth, C went up to my mother's room to kiss her goodnight. Coming down to some indignation meeting, "do go up and kiss her," she begged my sisters; "she longs for you to. Then you could talk it out." They could not, and she would soon learn why. Boarded out at Hill Street while our flat was fitted out, returning for some meal, "This isn't a hotel, you know," she was told. It was her turn to rush upstairs in tears. Later, cowardly, I walked *him* round the Park, and begged him to do something about it which, to judge by later experience, he must have bravely done. We had booked that flat on the eighth floor of a steel skeleton just off the Abbey Road. When the elevations went up they were in the shoddiest by-pass style, but there was a view over the whole of London. People then attacked such flats as immoral "blocks of immurement for single persons and birth-controllers", to quote a letter in *Country Life*. To us it was a nest in a tree-top.

I must now qualify as an architect. It had become a social as much as an aesthetic obligation under the influence of a stammering bundle of Welsh idealism called Trystan Edwards, who used to visit Oxford to publicize his bold scheme for a Hundred New Towns. I had joined a small class in the Ruskin School, run on elementary Froebel lines by Robert Goodden, which he had hoped would get us off the first year of the five-year course at the reputedly progressive AA School of Architecture in London. For me, starting in January, it did not. I found myself in an annexe with a roomful of very young delinquents doing remedial work. Schoolboy smut and stink bombs set the tone. After a term of this, which seemed to drag me back into a past I thought I had left for ever, I quietly left and apprenticed myself to A. S. G. Butler, a shy, donnish man with a small domestic and Catholic clientèle. He was a pupil and devotee of Lutyens. He taught us Style — or rather styles: he could do anything from Byzantine in the manner of Bentley to ecclesiastical Gothic in the manner of Pugin to Picturesque in the manner of Norman Shaw. His assistant, Humph, gave us the lowdown on flashings and dampcourses. It was just right, for a year or two during which I learnt still more by building ourselves a muddle of a house under the shrewd eye of a tactful foreman. But a country-house architect, which I could so easily have become, was not what I wanted to be. Leaving Butler's cosy office was an escape from the world which an architect from my background could be expected to inhabit. I joined two nice, high-minded young people, William and Aileen Tatton Brown, as a not-yet-qualified junior partner who might be expected to bring in some work, but really as a disciple. He had worked with Lurçat in Paris and with Lubetkin in London, and they had lately won a competition. This was the real thing. The only job I did bring in was that classic — a new wing for my aunt Zena's wistaria-covered Queen Anne Cottage in Berkshire. This we did in matching brick, but with a flat roof and plate-glass french windows. We made her a model, which she thought a sweet toy. But when she saw it full size, to her great embarrassment and misery, she had to sack me and get a builder to put on a tiled roof and Georgianize the windows. She was charming: I am sure I was intolerable.

Taking the RIBA's external exams (which students in schools of architecture were excused), by means of a low-grade correspondence course, was called the hard way. Educationally, it was certainly the wrong way. But it got me qualified in three years instead of five, and in the nick of time in 1939. This time I spent the prize money not on poetry but on the literature of the Modern Movement, and particularly on the complete works of Le Corbusier and Lewis Mumford. This was poetry to me.

Midway through this, I discovered my eyes were (as they say) on the blink. A Welbeck Street specialist, having first taken a few teeth out, took the view that the condition was tubercular and that I risked blindness unless I spent some months in a clinic at Davos. He finally agreed we could "live out" in the Alps, provided it was at the proper altitude. We heard that the conductor Furtwängler wished to let his cottage in the meadows between Pontresina and St Moritz. So in May, off we drove, with six-month-old Christopher, in a lovely dark-blue and white Renault convertible we had bought off its stand at the Motor Show. We climbed over the Julier Pass in a blinding snowstorm and descended into an earthly paradise. After some weeks, the eyes unchanged, we heard of the famous Dr Vogt in Zurich, so we went to see him. Very rare, he said, but not serious: stay out the summer, then forget it. In a lab. full of rabbits with eye ailments a girl did a meticulous water-colour drawing of my bad eye, then we drove back over the passes, free as air.

Acla Silva was a studio, with tiny bedrooms off it, steep-roofed, blue and white like the car, with a cock-eyed chimney. Meadows sheltered by pine forest, starred that June with a million flowers, sloped away to a little café called the Meierei, with the lake beyond, and the single rock peaks of the Engadine serially disposed as far as the western rim of the earth. At night the galaxies took over from the flowers. It was ideal territory for my kind of climbing, the scented mossy woods and ice-cold streams tempting me ever upwards. The narrow snow ridge of Piz Palu, with a rope of tourists, had nothing on Piz Julier with C or Piz Ot alone — beautiful 11,000-foot rock peaks that one could drift up in a day from our high valley. I never remember any effort, or ever meeting anybody: we seemed to have the heights to ourselves. Parents came for a few days, with seventeen-year-old Nancy in tow, in the hope she might "get over" her love for the man she soon married. For much longer we had Maury Heckscher, who had no sense of time and no egotism to upset his role of mirror reflecting our happiness. There are times when three is best company. We stayed till we could smell autumn in the air.

Chapter four

THE DURATION

―――――――――

IN THE MONTH I started work with Mr Butler it was already beginning. Jinny wrote to my father from Munich:

Gloomy people here think there may be a war between England and Italy. I don't listen to that sort of talk but it is a bit beastly it should be going on. Why is the world so arranged that a few dodderers who are nearly passing away from decrepitude, like Ramsay and Baldwin, and one enormous bloated chin like Musso, should have it in their power not only to ruin millions of very good lives but also to plunge European civilization into the bottomless pit? Why on earth can't people learn to live as individuals and not as nations? What the devil would you or I care if Musso planted his chin in the prickly soil of British Somaliland, wherever that may be? But, oh no, says Ramsay in a voice quaking with emotion or alternatively with old age – England (that glorious myth) calls and Lionel must go and hurl bombs on the Duomo in Florence. . . . If only people would leave each other alone. This is rather a specially nice world and we've only got a short time in it.

Any young creature of any sensibility must always feel this. In our case two influences reinforced our natural aversion from that world of Imperial Defence to which grandfather Esher had devoted so much thought and energy. The first was our father's. In reaction himself against Edwardian arrogance and the pomposity of powerful men, he enjoyed baiting them in newspaper articles and at dinner tables and making provocative and ill-informed speeches about armaments in the House of Lords. He now had a platform, and putting the hedonistic years behind him plunged into public life, his unorthodoxy forgiven him by most people because of his wit. "Is Hitler a Napoleon or a Joan of Arc?" he would ask; and for longer than most people, shocked by the vindictiveness of the French since Versailles, he was prepared to believe the second. There was also the influence of the affection they both felt, in his case sentimental, in hers inherited, for the Germans of the West and South. There unquestionably existed a relationship between the cultured aristocracy and the *haute bourgeoisie* of Munich and Vienna and their opposite numbers in England which did not exist with their French equivalents. Even at the ordinary tourist level the smiling Germans, anxious as ever to please, made a far better impression than the *insouciant* French, and were more reliable than the charming, feckless Italians. Of what was going to happen to the Jews we had no conception. Indeed in the early 1930s Heidegger, Niemöller and von Stauffenberg were all strong supporters of Hitler.

I was not myself pro-German, or anti-French, but I had an obsessive fear and horror of war, generated by the bitter literature of the 1914–18 holocaust. "The bomber will always get through," Baldwin asserted, and the image was of innocent populations burnt and choking on mustard gas and phosgene. Nobody should claim any special sensitivity in this matter. It was an accident that C and I fell under the charm of Dick Sheppard and the compulsiveness of his pacifist faith. I began to pray again, not to catch cricket balls, but for peace, progressively more hopeless though it seemed. Feeling as we did as a family, we conventionally supported Mr Chamberlain — he was a lot more enterprising than M. Daladier — and we took pride in his decency and his umbrella alongside posturing Hitler and Goering. Munich was our *memento mori*, striking with charnel-house chill as the family gathered, day after day with the regularity of mealtimes, for the ordeal of the BBC news. Such ups and downs of hope and fear were new in our experience, and nothing in the war would equal them for suspense. Not yet morally in uniform, we looked at the frantic trench-diggers and labelled children and gas masks in a mood of unspeakable desolation and tragedy. When the reprieve came, I could not go all the way with the Poet Laureate:

> As Priam to Achilles for his son,
> So you, into the dark, divinely led,
> To ask that young men's bodies not yet dead
> Be given from the battle not begun.

But I whole-heartedly shared the French view: *Ce n'est pas magnifique, mais ce n'est pas la guerre.*

★

Immediately after Munich, everybody started joining things. For me, immersed in architecture and out of touch with Beaumont Street opinion, it could only be the Fire Service: an architect, I piously believed, must protect, not destroy. This meant periodical training evenings with hook ladders and hose in some station up Kilburn way, in an atmosphere of total unreality. Indeed unreality was the note of the coming year. As it progressed to the inevitable climax we moved the children to Watlington, where county ladies were enthusiastically enrolling, calling on cottagers, running up blackout curtains, taping windows, laying in headlight masks and provisioning cellar shelters. Some superstition prevented our getting to work on this universal assumption: we resolutely took no action of any kind, continued to wander the landscape, tried not to yield to despair when fleets of black-painted bombers rumbled close overhead. When finally the call-up arrived, C took me to Slough station, where we parted by the entrance, the entrance I believed, to Armageddon. Months later, when I could contemplate it, I described that journey:

I am in a train, going up to London. The third-class carriage is crammed, but nobody speaks, and the dusk thickens, for it is the first night of the blackout. The elation and the misery are too deep for words, as the dusk thickens among the doomed, expectant houses, and minds and figures hurry to and fro. We know, as we sit quietly in a row, that we are embarked on what used to be called a journey into the unknown, and excitement goes some little way to cancel our unhappiness. The train jogs along, the peaceful machinery still functions, but behind it one hears a new noise, a sort of hum or murmur, like distant crowds cheering a coronation, as death resumes its power.

In fact, of course, nothing happened. Substation X was an underground garage off the Abbey Road, where we slept in rows against the wall on beds we fetched from home. It had a glass roof, so when the smoke or din of the canteen became intolerable one lay on one's bed in total darkness uncharacteristic of London, while torches and cigarettes went past, waiting for it to be late enough to sleep. Then the snoring chorus took over, bestial, meaningless, later to be a familiar experience to light sleepers like myself. In the daytime there were, of course, drills, and appliances (pumps drawn reassuringly by London taxis) to be polished, and, endlessly, sandbags to be filled. The war was still all rumour, false raid warnings, cars with Priority labels rushing about.

As time went on, personalities sorted themselves. In the social spectrum that stretched from barrister to chimney sweep a minority of Hampstead-fringe intellectuals, mainly Jewish, made life interesting. Some evenings, we read Shakespeare plays in the icy fug of the sandbag shelter. Others saw passionate political sessions in the canteen, when the Left minority sought to persuade the servile majority to assert itself. Officers, no-nonsense regulars, amused themselves on these occasions by ringing the alarm bells and watching the debaters, Right, Left and Centre, clatter out into the darkness and tumble into their taxis, wrestling with respirator strings, to be driven round the block in the rain or the moonlight.

Occasionally we were boarded out in small parties in evacuated houses. In the servants' quarters of the rich neo-Georgian mansions of Avenue Road, "kind tabby cooks" (as I then described them) gave us tea and toast by basement ranges. Here one had the luxury of an attic bedroom, and silence enough to lie awake and listen to the wind in the wires of the barrage balloons. One also had an infinity of time to think. As that dewy, golden autumn declined into winter, and still the bombers did not come, it began to dawn on me that I was no longer a pacifist. A letter from Maury, written after listening to the King's speech on the outbreak of war, made my moral isolation and physical inactivity in this prosperous suburb hard to justify and hard to endure.

I have heard indirectly that you have been feeling a kind of fatalism. Even if this is not true I know for myself what your attitude was while I was still in England — from your letter to me in Vienna and our talks together. I know your extreme horror of the irrationality and primitiveness of war and that it could easily lead to such a fatalism, — a belief that you and people like yourself have no part in a world which must resort to such barbaric means. In all humility (because I write still from the peaceful woods of Little Moose), I beg you not to believe it. To me and to all who know you, you are not only an instance but nearer the essence of the things for which this war is fought. If America, as I believe and hope it will, should join, it would be with the end that men like you and ideals such as yours should survive. Our tragedy is that we should be forced by circumstance to use methods so contrary to our beliefs. But such a discrepancy need not lead to fatalism. Men like yourself have a large part even in this brutal and senseless world that begins today.

Then came the heroic resistance of the Finns to the Russian invasion, which made it painfully clear to us laggards that there is such a thing as a just war. Most compelling of all was the feeling that one is not entitled to adopt a posture of moral superiority to one's friends. Who was I to refuse to "take life", since this was my generation's destiny? The war existed and I wanted it won. So at Christmas I left London and looked for a job in the Army.

Volunteers badgering recruiting offices were a mere nuisance at that time — grit in the wheels of conscription — and it was not until May that 979029 Gunner Brett walked through the gates of Preston Barracks in Brighton. At that moment the Germans drove into France and we were locked in for intensive drilling and conditioning, for the clipping of our wings, until it was thought safe to take us out for beach defence. C saved coupons for the long drive from Watlington, and we were allowed to speak through the railings, which we lined like animals in a zoo. In mid-June the gates opened and we marched out into the blinding light of that brilliant summer. Unreality became surrealist as we built our sandbag fort at Black Rock Pool, all among the bathing belles and the strolling, red-faced, still unconscripted crowds. The most expendable soldiers in England, we had a World War One Lewis Gun pointed out to sea. One moonlight night, after a red alert, a jumpy officer actually saw German scouts creeping along a groyne. To the east, the white cliffs tangibly represented the fortress island, overhead were the wild scribbles of the Battle of Britain, and before long we learnt the unmistakable rhythm of German engines pounding over towards London or dropping the odd bombs if they were in trouble. Above our absurd *Beau Geste* fort was a modernistic block of empty luxury flats, in which C and another wife spent an occasional night overlooking the gasworks, while we slept out on the pavement below. Other nights

I was on guard [I wrote to C] on the edge of the cliffs (where we walked after dinner) from 9.30 to 12.30 and slept beautifully in the fort till 6.30, which is the first decent night since we've been down here. It was very beautiful on guard. One saw the millions of stars come out all over the sky, and humans gradually disappear from the face of the earth. The hissing sea below got darker and more mysterious, and a chain of little lights appeared along its horizon, which were probably the little patrol boats, which are sort of floating sentries. Occasionally one bawled "Halt! Who goes there!" to a passer-by, who jumped out of his skin and produced his identity card. On the edge of the cliff one had the feeling of guarding England itself — not some dreary arms dump or military post.

Such unpredictable moments of joy were heightened by the encircling gloom, as when we ate a superb lobster dinner with Jeremy Hutchinson, now a RNVR rating in HMS *King Alfred*, who within a month wrote to tell us he had married Peggy Ashcroft before joining Mountbatten in HMS *Kelly*, soon to sink off Crete. For four weeks we were moved to Rottingdean, where I called on bedridden Maurice Baring and had a kind of love-affair with Enid Jones's whole family in her golden book-lined room. War gave an extraordinary radiance to such interludes.

None of the heroics of 1940 affected my loathing of the war. This was a bad time for my mother who, like most Americans, was passionately patriotic:

This war is more terrible, and more glorious too, than the last — above all quite different. I wouldn't like you to miss entirely the thrill of that forlorn hope, that wonderful retreat on Dunkirk and across the sea, which brought out once again the shining English tenacity that refuses to acknowledge defeat. I remember that years ago in America, long before I ever knew that I should be one of them and learn to love them, I used to hear it said: "The English never know when they are beaten." But it is nobler than that — they know, but they *won't* give in. And when I say, this war is more glorious than the last I mean it has a sort of David-and-Goliath quality. Don't you feel it too? And so, out of all these defeats, victory will surely come. Old Browning (does your generation read him?) knew all about it. (Oh dear, I'm afraid this is very hackneyed.)

> "We fall to rise, are baffled to fight better,
> Sleep, to wake."

But what about you, my poor dear? From C one gets the impression that you have to work harder under more uncomfortable conditions than anyone hears of. I hope I may take that with a grain of salt. Do you really have to sleep on the *pavement*? No one else seems to do that! Nancy says John Shuckburgh enjoys his new military life and even gets time to play squash — and young Brown, whom I saw again the other day, seems quite gay and happy, has joined the regimental sports club etc., and comes home on Sundays. As they seem to be training you as an infantryman after all, it seems a pity now that you didn't join the County Regiment and stay at Cowley. So convenient.

Nancy says Evelyn is very unhappy, he feels his work is useless, and longs to join the army. She says he has grown to hate putting on his London clothes and white collar every day, and wishes every time it were a uniform! But they won't let him go. Naturally any high-spirited young man whose work keeps him in moderate safety outside the army must feel this now, and one honours him for it. He feels it more, now that you and his brothers have gone.

You heard about Patrick Baring? He was a sweet boy, unpretentious and brave — we shall miss him very much. He was only 21.

In response to this last I quoted four lines —

> Display no more in vain the lofty banner;
> For see, where on the bier before ye lies
> The pale, the fall'n, the untimely sacrifice
> To your mistaken shrine, to your false idol, Honour.

And I added:

The lines I quote were written by a Lady Winchelsea (I think) in the 17th cent. She, of course, was writing of wars long since forgotten, and the various honourable motives which prompted the grandees to make those wars forgotten too. Looking back, the "honour" of Henry V, of Louis XIV, of Chatham and Palmerston seems poor reason for wars like the 100 years, the 7 years or the Crimea. But the "untimely sacrifices" were made, gladly, thousands and thousands of times.

Do send me anything you would like me to read, but you can see how at this time certain things might mean more to you than to me.

This was depressing enough, but in a determined effort to shock, worse was to come.

> Three quarters of the men here have no opinion of any interest and more or less believe their newspaper. The remaining quarter may be said to think this:
>   1. The war is due partly to the jealousy and ambition of the Germans, partly to the Jews, who are held responsible for half the evils in the world because of their control over business, newspapers, cinemas etc.
>   2. The only hope for Europe is domination by England.
>   3. France at the end of the war must be made part of the British Empire.
>   4. War responds to a natural human instinct and it is not possible or desirable to get rid of it.
> Now you'll see that if in the above one substitutes Germany for England, one gets the four cardinal points of Nazism. If one points this out and asks "If England became openly Nazi (i.e. declared their ideas instead of keeping them dark), and if England acted on these ideas as the Nazis have done, would you still fight for England?" The answer is: "I would fight for England whatever happened, right or wrong." There is the fifth cardinal point of Nazism.

I come badly out of this correspondence, this skirmish in the long campaign which Jinny had fought years ago and from which I had until now held aloof. It was at last my turn to smash to pieces, without mercy, the image of the dutiful son.

As the summer faded Brighton sea-front emptied and grew shabby. Shops put up the shutters; sandbags leaked and spilled; old newspapers slid downwind or tangled in the ubiquitous barbed wire; rubbish accumulated in corners. Tedium and beer-swilling took over as the regiment pulled back into winter quarters. Escape came at last as a posting to an OCTU in the North. On the way, a week's leave. The countryside as we drove freely out of Brighton struck my senses as though for months I had been blinded by the glare of the sea. Brown-tiled villages and grey towers were embosomed in enormous statuesque elms and umber beeches, all at their darkest before they began to turn. The Sussex landscape, says my diary, "purrs like an old cat". We had to learn how to handle a week's leave, how to fill it with loving recognition of people and things but still keep the detachment which would make its end tolerable, to forget the army and the war but stay subconsciously aware of them, so that one could return to them with the least possible suffering. This was a comparatively easy one, with a new experience ahead.

The war, for us, now entered its long middle period. From a nightmare it settled into a life-style. 123 OCTU at Catterick Camp, after that low-grade, low-morale training regiment, seemed a marvel of good sense and efficiency.

In the elemental landscape of the North Riding, where rock is thinly clad in shreds of soil and scrub, where only two seasons, summer and winter, exist, only two attitudes to the war were possible, and I learnt to accept and then fully inhabit the one I had chosen. This is when the public schools come into their own, since finally all one has to do is to revert to type. It is not a question of learning anything new, but rather of abandoning the pose of being grown-up. Two other things helped enormously. One was that gunnery had a quite refined technique which in the abstract it was impossible not to enjoy first learning and then teaching. The other was that the place, in those early post-Dunkirk days, had a sense of dedication, directly inspired by that same sense in its Colonel, Hardress Waller. At Brighton I had learnt to interpolate talk with four-letter words and to loot absent people's property without the slightest sense of shame. From him I learnt how a single person can transform the atmosphere of the world he moves in, and how such leadership alone makes war endurable.

It has been said that "the course of every intellectual, if he pursues his journey unflinchingly enough, ends in the obvious, from which the non-intellectuals have never stirred". This had been my course. But he cannot just sit there, accepting the universe. So into the vacuum, through two long northern winters, stepped Post-War Reconstruction. Up with Uthwatt! Down with the RA! Backing up Abercrombie, getting to work on Reith, soft-pedalling Ansell, encouraging Keynes, inventing Peace Terms, Prefabricated Houses, Multi-level Business Precincts, new uses for Watlington, for rubble, for artists, my father and I kept up a hell-for-leather crackpot correspondence, a period piece if ever there was one.

From William Tatton Brown, until he was posted to India, came letters more specifically architectural, with diagrams of how new material might be stitched into the fabric of cities, now considerably moth-eaten by the bombing. All over England, as the war got into its long stride, isolated friends, starved of mental stimulus, began writing, sharing after-the-war fantasies, exchanging signals through the blackout.

We rented a grey terrace house in a steep cobbled street in Richmond and moved the family up before the first of two savagely cold winters immobilized us, and the landscape settled into its four-month monochrome. We looked east over the richly wooded banks of the Swale to Easby Abbey, a Turneresque view, very blue in the winter dusk. By contrast, two women next door appeared to be burying a baby in their yard. Ours held a few hens, cosseted by our buxom maid, Nellie, from Beer in Devon. Most evenings I could come home to a firelit nursery, but at ten or so I must set off on the two-mile torchlit tramp to Bourlon Lines, steel-rimmed boot-soles ringing on the tarmac, with identical footsteps before me and behind. There I would join a score of snoring cadets in an echoing barrack room that smelt of sweat and floor polish. Lying awake, I would brood on how dull I had become, stripped of the ideas and artefacts by means of which I had once been identifiable. "In my dullness and weakness," I wrote, "I envy the majority of good soldiers, who have put their best into *themselves*. They act by instinct, not by thought. In the morning they sing. Through the day they work steadily, like horses. At night they lie down and sleep, never awake in the darkness. Poets salute such people, but cannot be like them: to see, and to be, that's asking too much."

Except for one nightmare train journey through the Christmas blackout to Watlington, with the three children parked on the luggage racks while the rest of us stood, we took our leaves in the Lakes, summer and winter. Here was that same radiance of all wartime escapes. An evening on Windermere. . . .

The tiny pointed skiff floats in the middle of the lake, a mist rises from the silent oily water, high enough to blur the bases of the woods and hills but not to touch their broken outlines, which attract the eye, sharp against the gold sky, in which the gold sun slides down. We two float, together but each alone, paddling with hands at intervals to keep the bow into the sun which draws us like a flame,

Grandpa Heckscher   Grandpa Esher

The Roman Camp

Aunt Doll ("Brett")

Aunt Sylvia of Sarawak

My mother

Aunt Zena (Dare)

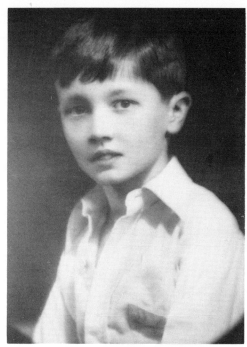

Nursery

Prep School

Four Selves

University

Profession

"C"

because elsewhere greyness encroaches. The silence is so perfect that we name the single sounds, voices and laughter from a boat a mile away, chorus of birdsong from the remote banks on either hand, a motorbike, a church clock. Now a fish plops, punkies skate, a small bug spirals madly on the surface. Drops from raised oars fall regularly, making entwining circles. We float on, while the mist rises, the sun bites into the skyline, and the hearts of women on the bank go out to our twin silence, our tininess, our feelings they share.

One day I swam across to a wooded island and wandered naked on tufted grass among the secret trees. A hot wind ruffled the tarn, misted the Coniston hills. Another day we rowed in a grey boat to a sunbaked reedy bay where wild yellow iris grew. The mountains sank behind the trees, a grey tripper steamer passed at intervals. There was no darkness, or cold, or rain, but orange umbrellas, the stone balustrade, beyond which laburnum, azalea and copper beech, the silver lake, the piled up receding hills. This for rest. And for effort, the crazy terrifying rocks — Pavey Ark, Middlefell Buttress, Gimmer Crag. Tommy Clark is solid, never apprehensive, assumes success. While he sits above, indicating holds, I in alternate contempt for the easiness of the climb and quaking terror at its delicacy, go through all the emotions, all forgotten in the moment when I land beside him. Then in the scented evening C and I walk to our bedroom in the birchwood, and lying under single sheets look up at Corot's foliage in the fading sky.

Before passing out as officers we had to do a month with a regular regiment. Mine was with 12 RHA in the Fens — "a hard and desolate month", I noted.

Chatteris, shapeless yellow houses and innumerable pubs — planless, squat, islanded in the plain of black mould and sickeningly straight ditches. Landscape devoid of all mystery, efficient tool of a race of stolid and utterly prosperous farmers. Black geometry, into which lonely brick cubes dip and slowly sink. Flatness, flatness of spirit, yet in this desert certain humans are fated to live, among them Mrs H, fragile pathetic type of 20th-century civilization, struggling (but there must be no evidence of struggle) to keep up appearances, to keep a maid, in whose clean but desolate house I spent this month. Husband, always in the pub, polite boys who kept white rabbits, ritzy looking wireless set, heavy three-piece suite in the lounge (still being paid for) — panic and emptiness. It was good, with the help of a visit from C, to cheer up Mrs H — better than the bleak Mess, with wireless blaring all day and hunting men nodding over the *Field* in deck chairs. Their escape was a day at Newmarket races, mine to Cambridge, to that world that had so soon and so inaccessibly become the past. Some of the time we spent on one of those vast, confused, deliberately miserable Exercises that punctuated army life in England. In a pitiless east wind we lived two days on dog biscuits, two nights standing beside our drivers, asleep vertically. Ely cathedral's single tower was always there on the horizon, unnoticed.

After two years at Catterick, now as an instructor training one troop after another of keen, anxious young cadets, I longed to escape from what had become a rather bourgeois, if austere, routine. A staff course was predictably offered me, but I refused it, determined not to follow in my father's flat footsteps. I applied for what was called the Air O.P., a group of officers who were to fly slow Austers over the battlefield to observe the fall of shot, but was rejected on an eye test. The real shortage, I was told, was of ordinary gunner officers on the ground, which I was in the job of producing. A dropout from educational and social privilege, I consequently remained for the duration a round peg in a very square hole, like many others. (My father, energetically supported by John Betjeman and Kenneth Clark, had occupied some of the Phony War with a scheme for the secret exemption from active service of a carefully compiled list of 50 artists, writers and musicians, but it was inevitably turned down by the Secretary of State for War.)

But finally my battery commander, Dick Streatfeild, got command of a new Field Regiment forming up north, and asked me to go with him as its adjutant. So it was goodbye to family life in Richmond. After a month in the Durham coalfield, receiving 25-pounders and equipment and people, we were into exercises in the Cleveland Hills. I was at the point where upward strains met downward stresses, and it was my job to see that orders which I could not always understand or justify were carried out by strong-willed and sometimes recalcitrant battery commanders senior to and older than myself. These points of pressure are critical to army cohesion, and are interesting, if arduous, to occupy. At least I knew more or less what was going on. And against lack of sleep, loss of temper, cold of motorcycling on frosty nights, one had to set the undeniable pride of being part of this splendid display of force, the odd interlude in a remote country house, the final dirty, exhausted return march and the cosy sense of something behind one. Yet these splendid displays of force were also hateful. It was hateful to see lawns cut to pieces by tracked vehicles, secret places violated by barbed wire. "We clatter through sensible coherent streets on tanks and motorbikes like Attila through Rome. The integrity that bound men and land and home together has been taken away. Infesting the disordered landscape over which the Spitfires roar I feel oppressed by the recurring, tiresome phrase — the times are out of joint."

Even so, physical stresses of battle school or firing camp seemed any day preferable to the interminable evenings in the mess in a hutted camp in Northumberland or in the curtainless carpetless drawing-rooms of Victorian villas on the fringes of industrial cities. Here the mental strains of personalities suppressed in the interest of community life were almost audible. But long training in football field and dormitory now paid off, and we somehow got along together. Leeds and Bradford, with their magnificent black buildings, absorbed the dinginess of war more easily than the south, and were worth getting to know. Through the kindness of new friends, particularly the Behrens family, I got as mixed up as I could with the musical and intellectual life of Bradford and gave lectures on post-war reconstruction to the Rotarians, the YMCA and the local society of architects. C came gallantly up for weekends in which every hour counted. Station hotels and freezing rectories received us. Pale-grey neo-classic houses in derelict gardens on the steppes of the Cheviots we cruelly white-washed into military order, while the seasons revolved, each with its own kind of sadness.

These were the years of love-in-absence, when the lost art of letter-writing was restored to us. We expressed love in a thousand ways, in frantic plots for last-moment leave, in midnight partings on station platforms, in heartache and drink and stoicism, in endless, endless letters and poems. Springs had special poignancy, children a super-natural beauty, and we had exaggerated visions of the bliss of unmitigated domestic life. But above all we were forced to feel by having to write. A day containing nothing worth mentioning showed up as a sinful waste of life, and there is no doubt that when the war ended, and with it this discipline, there were more such days; but they passed unnoticed.

I relieved one lonely evening by an exercise in purest nostalgia.

Watlington in July. This year I only had a single day there, coming back north from Larkhill, and it rained ceaselessly through a dank mist, while in the dark and friendly library (that wonderful background for talk) we discussed whether we would ever live there after the war. How I have hated and loved this house, this place. I see it most often in July, in high summer. Silent and golden (after London) evenings of July, when the great limes of the park rise like enormous full-rigged ships at anchor, at whose feet little specks of rabbits sit like gulls on a grassy sea, or (to spoil the illusion) skip in a circle and change places, lit by the long paths of declining sun. Not a leaf flutters. I walk along the balustrade, while the women (the beautiful and interesting women, for it is the beginning of a house party) are all bathing and sitting in front of mirrors. It is very warm and there is no sound but cooing pigeons. The woods are completely mysterious and impenetrable, for the sun has left them all but the higher treetops. The garden is melancholy, finished with for the day, and waits to be revived by the dew. In the kitchen, operations are reaching a climax; the table is loaded with bowls of cream and flour and the corpse of the "garden rabbit" which I put there (triumphantly) not long ago. The long dining-room table glitters and Allen is lighting the candles. (Desmond is here, and Ruby Lindsay, and perhaps Gerry Villiers.) The house is a hive of diverse activity, soon to be concentrated by the gay ring of the bell and the gathering for dinner (I'm late); but outside the world is silent (a car changes down on Howe Hill), the fields are deserted, the landscape is folded for the night.

The night is shut out. It is not allowed to invade, but footmen fasten the solid Georgian windows, the wooden shutters, the heavy velvet curtains. Stronger barriers of talk and music are interposed. Occasionally lovers will escape (it is soft and warm; lights move on the plain) to walk over Watlington Hill; or C in a white lace dress will twirl and dance alone on the terrace. But the house is securely fastened, the cushions and tennis racquets are brought in, and night is shut out.

The morning is radiant and my yellow room is full of glare. We get up so late that we miss the freshness, the awakening, and we step out of the green-shaded library into full day. In the loggia are bowls of raspberries, nectarines, figs. The girls are late and lazy, the young men stiff with sleep. Light cascades into the clearings, sun filters into the thickets, but the woods are such a tangle of briars and willowherb that no one enters them; the fields are sun-scorched, the lanes are overgrown and impassable, for the landscape is in the grip of extravagant July, and its growth and fertility are out of our control. The birds are bemused and silent and the woods are unexplored.

Now is the time to lie full length and let the scarlet sun press on your eyelids, then to plunge arms into a damp pile of mown grass (the motor-mower can be heard going backward and forward on the north side). Now to escape in sandals and shorts and let the bracken brush your legs, where clouds of flies float in sunlight, but the dew still lies in the shade. The wind of the slopes caresses, and right up to the horizon the fields are white and gold. The sun is mounting; the cows get into the shade (imagine the snow now, and the rattling of the bare branches . . . there may be a war). Let me escape and climb this easy tree, and sway hidden among the beech-leaves; then I will run down the slope and creep past the farm unseen, and penetrate into clearings where no one has ever been before. (A maddening bomber passes overhead.) Deeper and deeper one can go, till the wood closes in and no shred of sky indicates the ordinary world. The light is the dark green of the sea-bed, in which stand the thin grey shafts of beeches, thickening into the distance. Between them may approach . . . what? A god? A girl? Those shy deer, or some terrifying beast, heard before seen? But the silence is profound. No lonely, primeval bodger chips his pegs, no keeper prowls. Only a small white owl goggles at me from a dead stump, hinting without a flicker of an eyelid that I am unwelcome.

1944, we now knew, would be our year of action, and outside connections and escapist activities began to fall away.

Today Winston inspected us in a snowstorm. He appeared round a corner in the General's car. We started cheering. Then suddenly the procession stopped. The old man in his square bowler struggled out rather decrepitly and climbed into an armoured truck where he sat high up in the back like a Buddha and drove past at walking pace, making his silly V-sign. I think he is becoming a bit of a menace. But it was gallant of him to do it in the freezing cold.

I enjoyed this last exercise enormously. It snowed and hailed and rained and fogged and I never felt cold for a moment. I had a wonderfully cosy night in my tiny bivouac tent, with the rain pelting down on it.

At last that endless winter, in which the pins moved with such desperate slowness up the map of Italy, melted into its magnificent spring, and our turn came. Everything was a deadly secret, the move to the south coast, the waterproofing of our vehicles, the briefings in Sussex country houses in May weather of distracting beauty. Even now, reading of Tolstoy's last years, I was not entirely cut off from my old self:

Shall I go on as I am or forsake all and follow him? Am I on the wrong track *now*? Ought I to be here, waiting to join in the killing among people whose point of view I have never shared? Too late: the train moves on, leaving the little wayside station behind.

And so the long-awaited moment at last arrived. "Send officer to . . . for orders 1800 hours today."

Chapter five

FEAR THIS NO MORE

WE HAD BEEN sunbathing on Lancing beach, looking into the glare towards France, but now our orders were to turn tail and head inland to Tilbury. I led the Regiment* on the long march through the heavy June foliage and the miles of South London. In the poorer parts (never in the middle-class areas) we were showered with sweets, buns, soap, then, after a sleepless night in camp listening to the first buzz-bombs motoring close overhead, and wondering what the hell they were, we embarked in a brand-new American LST.

The last thing we saw on dry land [I wrote to C next day] was a little row of slum cottages, covered with decorations and little flags, whose whole population, old and young, turned out to cheer us by.

We are now at anchor, under a cloudless sky, while the huge forest of ships assembles, each with its silver balloon. Through field glasses we recognize the signs of units we know on other ships, and wave at them. It is a silvery armada, the only dots of bright colour being the strings of little signal flags that flutter from each mast. In its laconic, modern way it is an intensely romantic scene, as vivid as a Canaletto under the sparkling sun.

We share the officers' mess and cabins. The officers are lanky, in tight trousers; each has a pair of huge signed photographs of his girl (Hollywood style) built into his steel desk. The food, served by superb young negroes dressed in white, with long, loose-hanging arms, is wonderful (ice cream, asparagus tips, grapefruit). We in our dirtiest battle dress, prepared for every kind of filth and horror, were *not* prepared for this. We sit and stuff like children at a party, to the amusement of our hosts. When they go out, we plot to seize the ship, make the crew and the colonel walk the plank, and sail her to some palmy island, eating ourselves silly on this canned Lotus food.

*This role had its reverses. I was never allowed to forget the day in a remote corner of Normandy when I caught up with a truck which I saw with horror was the tail end of our mile-long convoy.

Three days later "here we are, stuck on this damned landing-craft, at anchor off the beach and bobbing about like a cork, unable to land because of the huge seas that are running. We have already been 48 hours like this, seesawing wildly, and the American food is uneatable. The men huddle in corners like sick hens and there seems no reason why we should *ever* leave this boat. In fact we laugh at ourselves like hell." Nothing, we felt, that might happen on dry land could be worse than this, and it was a delight finally to splash ashore.

The year that followed provided samples of most of the primeval terrors and instincts of mankind, yet to many was too personal in its impact to be communicable. Each had his special dread — the tank commander of being caught in a wood at dusk, the infantryman of rising to his feet in an airstream singing with death, the solitary gunner OP of wandering into a minefield or into the silence that in war is always sinister — and each had his moments of private fear, revulsion, frustration, exhilaration.

This campaign was exceptionally rich in the last ingredient, though it is difficult to write of alongside the massacres of the innocent and the deaths of friends. But to land in the bridgehead, to be in Bayeux for the first 14th of July, to break out into the bosky unscarred countryside of Normandy, to pound the German war machine to pieces in the Falaise pocket, and then to take part in the liberation of France and Belgium — these were not just historical incidents; they were profoundly moving experiences. Liberation was still a clean word (it was not till that winter that to "liberate" meant to "loot") and when I read a notice in a Brussels shop window:

TO THE SOLDIERS OF THE UNITED NATIONS
THANK YOU
FOR THE COMPLETE LIBERATION OF OUR DEAREST BELGIUM

I thought of my companions of Beaumont Street, lost in Italy, in Africa, in the air over the Channel five years ago already, and felt that this was their moment. The past and the future sharpened to such single points of time that summer.

Normandy, dewy, dusty, smelling of life one moment and death the next, seemed for a few weeks the crowded capital of the free world. Innumerable coloured signs pointed to the hideouts of friends, and in the intervals of battle a great deal of calling took place, until the whole field galloped off over the skyline and the bridgehead relapsed into the obscurity of base units and lines of communication. We were never again to be so concentrated either in space or in sentiment.

The job of an infantry division in the attack is to punch the hole through which the armour can ride on into the blue. Ours in the 15th Scottish Division in those last days of June was not so satisfying. Whatever it set out to achieve, it was later claimed to have been a strategic diversion, designed to bring down upon us the whole of the German armour, so that the Americans could achieve their breakout in the west. This it certainly did. A few days before it began

> We were close to a lovely little stone Renaissance château. I did some sightseeing, much to the suspicion of the occupying troops. Suddenly one felt oneself back in 1935 or so, with a two-seater just down the road with G.B. on it; trying to make out the date of a gateway, noticing the classic ilexes and the thin, fuzzy-topped French elms, which are quite unlike the flat English kind.
>
> Wherever we go we tread on the heels of the Germans and find their possessions lying about. A letter, for instance, beginning "My darling Tony, Yesterday you were with me; today already you seem so terribly far away. I hope you had a good journey and are comfortable. I feel this week will go slowly . . ." and so on. These sort of things make us all remember we are pacifists at heart, real *haters* of war. But we remind ourselves of the inhuman look of these young robots created by Hitler and know that they must be killed, and the girl's heart broken.

And so we went into the battle we had rehearsed for so many years. Counter-attacked by monstrous Tiger tanks, I remembered that inside them were the little boys who had marched and sung in the early sunlight below my window a dozen summers ago.

Ten days later, having consolidated our costly bridgehead over the Odon,

> It is a quiet night, with only a few guns popping irregularly and far more noise made by the fiendish atmospherics on my two wireless sets. Rarely I am woken up by a sudden voice saying "Victor target, Victor target, Victor target" over the air — and I must get busy and throw the guns into some sudden wild outburst of fire, springing up

from all points of the countryside as hundreds of guns join in, turning night into day and shaking earth and sky more furiously than the wildest thunderstorm. For a few minutes the beautiful and powerful orchestra of gunfire plays fortissimo; the rhythm is crazily exciting and there is every variety of note from the cymbal-clash of our own guns in this field (one of them just through the hedge unfortunately blows my lamps out whenever it fires) to the deep drums in the distance. The flashes light the leaves like dancing flames; the earth trembles. Then suddenly the storm dies, the echoes ripple away. "Stand easy," we send out to the gunners, and in the quiet dark they again wrap themselves in their blankets and are immediately asleep.

We all affect some degree of toughness, and being human find a lot in war to laugh at. But behind the gay air, the laughter, one sees so often in the people around one the serious air of peace, and love waiting patiently for its expression, and the unrecognized longing to create. And then somebody is killed, like John Hichens today. He was with me at Catterick, was 22, was just married to a girl who had been at Oxford with him — a lovely, serious, polite young man. And the awful thing is — one eats one's dinner, as big a dinner as usual, and the ripple dissolves. That is the horror of it.

We were pulled out for a few days, and on the 15th of July

I had a lovely day yesterday — managed to get into Bayeux. Every house had its tricolour, that lovely flag which I find so much more moving and romantic than the Union Jack. The red, white and blue stood out gaily against the old pale-grey houses, in a wonderful confusion of blobs and splashes down the narrow streets.

Outside the cathedral is the office where the refugees from the destroyed villages are brought to find a home. Very shabby lorries driven by boys of 15 honk through the crowd. Inside, the whole family, all its generations, sitting on the rescued sofa, with bundles and bicycles strapped on, the old women mutely resigned, the girl of 17 upright, conspicuous, the children having a marvellous treat. A very efficient young woman, Parisian type, not the rough Norman, in khaki Free French uniform and black beret, jumps on the running board and shouting to the boy driver leads the lorry out of sight.

This war is *not* a Crusade. We entered on it reluctantly and sadly, to save ourselves from conquest, after a series of terrible blunders. We have not the same sense of a mission as the enemy. And whether the war can ever do enough good to blot out its evil remains to be seen. No, my feeling in Bayeux cathedral and all the time is not that I am part of a movement — it's just a personal adventure to me.

I went into Caen the other day. If I have seemed to enjoy this war in any of my letters, I take it all back: one must *not*, ever, pretend to treat as a game or an adventure anything so terrible. There is nothing there, nothing for acres, but heaps of stone and splintered wood, gaunt obelisks of wall or chimney, standing one behind another like miniature dolomites into the distance (on to which the sun, among white clouds, goes on shining). Bulldozers have shoved a way through the rubble, where a street ran, over which you lurch crazily in your jeep. Civilians poke about in the rubble; young women push wheelbarrows with their blankets and feather beds; there are all the incongruous little details always revealed by blitz — but done by *us*, you see, by us to our friends: that is what is so terrible, and makes it impossible for me to call gaily "Bonjour, Madame" as I pass the widow with the shopping basket, or even to smile without embarrassment when I drive past the women pushing their belongings, though *they* smile, incredibly. It is so frightful that we, the "liberators", have had to be so destructive, and that our main weapons all along have been the horribly inhuman bomber and the creeping, searing barrage, which tears up the apple orchard and blows the cottage roof into the air. So this lovely, mature little city, with its eighteenth-century avenues, its Norman abbeys, its little grey squares, is now mostly indistinguishable from the East End of London, except that the rubble is a prettier colour.

Our dreams are mostly of good food, of silence, of the huge beech reaching up to the sun, with a pigeon in it, or a squirrel. And one dreams of a real life again, of extraordinary contacts with people, of art and talking about it, of odd evenings, of driving in the car to stay a weekend, of sailing with Christopher. I dream of you, interesting, thin, nobly beautiful, trying to do right. But of course we all dream of good food mostly.

The Normandy battles ended at Falaise, the arena selected for the destruction of von Rundstedt's armies. Here, as far as we could see, was

Nazism blown to pieces, its great toys of war reduced to violently twisted scrap-iron. The devastation stretched mile after mile — a scene out of H. G. Wells — the destruction of the Martians. There followed the day we had dreamed of:

> Except perhaps for the day of peace itself this was for me the great day of the war. On this day we saw the powers of darkness driven away, driven out by the hard struggle and discipline and the lovely devotion of all the simple little people in the world, by the students and shopkeepers, the parted lovers, the girls in mackintoshes, the ordinary run of peaceful, humorous, lazy humanity — and there they were, all down the road, touchingly anxious that we should realize their happiness and gratitude. I wish you could have stood beside me, high up in the air in my half-track, and shared our triumph. So many things to laugh at and cry over: the man in the blue uniform and brass helmet who jumped aboard and insisted on guiding us through his village, the girl who seeing us approach tore back into her garden, driven by a wild impulse, grabbed her biggest dahlias and tore back (she was too late for me but gave them to the blushing R.S.M. in the next truck), the little bands that struck up as one went by, the tired, terribly tired refugees who smiled and waved at every truck, the tricolour everywhere.
>
> It is they, the poor, who are so wonderfully generous and give us all they have. The rich are not seen. The poor will open their whole small house to you: the rich will (if asked) let you use the stables.
>
> When we arrived in our last town, the first thing we saw, whitewashed in huge ten-foot symbols on the wall, was the sinister symbol of the S.S.

$$\text{⚡⚡}$$

> Next day I passed the monstrous sign again. But by now some soldier had come with a little bit of chalk, and roughly written

FEAR   ⚡⚡   THIS
NO   MORE

It was about now that C, urged to do so by Donald McCullough of the BBC when she read him one of them, had begun to read my letters on the radio. I saw it as a way to hear her voice. But when I found myself writing inevitably with publication in mind (as in this last, I suppose) and when friends and others in the regiment discovered the secret, we stopped the series. I had in fact only one friend at RHQ who spoke my language and shared my style of joke — a very young, very unmilitary archaeologist called Harry James of Neath, Glamorgan, later a pillar of the British Museum. Ours was a defensive pact in face of our too highly motivated, will-driven colonel, who, when we had a couple of days' rest in a back area after some battle, would insist on a full day of regimental sports as "good for morale". It was my job to issue the intensely unpopular orders.

We found the Belgians *en fête* — their welcome undiluted by injured pride at having to be rescued by the Anglo-Saxons. Their richly royal tricolour had a different beauty, and of course Brussels for a month or two (until it had to retreat into a wretchedly heatless, meatless winter) became every soldier's bonanza. But in Holland we got in every sense bogged down. In those rickyards below the shivering poplars, in those long thatched farmhouses afloat on their seas of mud, we had to face the fact that it was autumn, that we had failed to secure the Arnhem corridor, that we were stuck. Germans, so recently a rabble escaping on farm horses and bicycles, suddenly became formidable again, endlessly resourceful, grimly returning to murder newly-freed villagers. Through October and November and into December we shuttled about the gluepot of the Rhine delta, marvellous defensive terrain because of its network of canals, hopeless for armour, laboriously clearing it of Germans, village by booby-trapped village, town by town — dark, frustrating, demoralizing days.

Let me tell you (this tea is surprisingly inspiring) what I have been feeling the last few weeks. First of all a great deal of disillusion and even despair about the world and the future. The silly quarrels between people who *must* be friends, the tactlessness and suspicion, the lack of vision (of course everyone is tired and bad-tempered: one must allow for that). The terrifying drop in moral standards (the delight in killing, the looting and universal ransacking of empty houses are not pretty). Worst of all, perhaps, the humorous and stolid cynicism which greets you if you suggest to Thomas Atkins that if he will but take an interest and demand the world he wants he

can get it. He doesn't believe in anything or feel the faintest con-
fidence or even interest in the possibility of improving our condition.

But then you find yourself loving him. In a moment it is another
mood, of extraordinary happiness. I have felt this a great deal lately. It
is poetic, irrational, impossible to describe — except that you must
know it; do you? An urge to throw off all cleverness and silliness,
and merely to give, oneself, everything, quite simply. What I have
liked about war has been that it has stripped one of all possessions and
responsibilities and left the spirit simple and bare. It's a little draughty
at times and when you aren't feeling well it's unbearable—but gosh it
makes you understand the Christian principle that a rich man hasn't a
hope of the kingdom of heaven: you have to be so very truthful and,
in a sense, to have nothing to give but yourself.*

We have been given printed instructions that no British soldier will
speak to a German except to give him or her an order, that we are not
to shake hands with them or enter their houses or restaurants or
cinemas, etc. etc. Moreover the GOC has addressed all officers of the
division and said that he hopes we are all firm supporters of the
Vansittart policy, that "there are *no* good Germans, only bad Germans and worse Germans". This being official policy, you can
imagine that the more junior officers will do very little to prevent the
country being smashed up from end to end. Now it may be right
(though it is probably not practicable) to put the German population
in Coventry to show them what the civilized world thinks of what
they have done: it's a new idea, anyway. But you can imagine how
little the official indoctrination appeals to people like me. Can Europe
ever settle down if we are to go on, long after the war is over,
stimulating hatred and fear? One realizes that *during* a war one's
personal morality can no longer be applied politically; but when it is
over one hoped to be able to resume civilized notions of right and
wrong. Let us definitely make it *impossible* for the Germans to make
another war; but within those limits we ought to cease hating and
search high and low for good Germans, revolutionary Germans,
who will clean up the country from top to bottom and put it back on
the road it lost a hundred years ago.

In the last week of November we had finally cleaned out Holland up

*Taking this line with Cyril Connolly on some mid-war leave in London, I was taken
down a peg. "You think there's some virtue in standing in a fish-queue."

to the Maas and fired our first rounds across the river into Germany. There we dug in just before the frosts came, with the enemy in easy view on the opposite bank. The autumn battles were over, the tracks were hard, and visiting was resumed. Victor Balfour, my hiking companion in the Thuringian Forest a dozen years ago, was now Brigadier (BGS) at 8 Corps Headquarters, on his way to a brilliant military career, and invited me to join his staff, which I said I would gladly do when the war ended. Another day, "determined to forge some link between the past and the future and for a change to set eyes on someone out of both", I called on Jo Grimond.

There he was, working in a dreary headquarters surrounded by people completely unlike himself so that he seemed a different animal, a noble beast in a farmyard. He was the same, elusive, shrewd, as difficult to grasp as quicksilver, kind, vague, humorous. It was lovely to talk on one's own level, and to have to make no allowances. Unfortunately we were both too busy to spare more than an hour. He is going to stand as a Liberal for the Shetlands and Orkneys or something very typical — anyway the sort of queer constituency that usually returns Liberals, so he will probably get in.

I had some heavenly *skating* today, right in the front line. An old moated castle, troops clattering in and out, carriers moving about and disturbing the unearthly silence (rather like an English Sunday morning) that you will always find in the front line if there isn't a battle on. You come on this scene, quite normal, and suddenly the whole atmosphere is changed because round and round the grim old castle are whirling little blobs of colour, boys, girls, gliding along like bubbles on a stream, round and round. It is such an oddity to find any civilians as far forward as this that everyone stops and stares; but they go on skating, gliding, quite unconcerned, angelic creatures out of another world, out of real life.

Oddly enough I am not the least bit homesick for England. It is *you* I want. But I am absolutely at home in Europe and could be perfectly happy if I never saw England again. My war, in fact, is not for England, but for Europe.

Early in that December the CO had told me he wished to train up an adjutant to replace me in due course and asked me to take a troop. My battery commander would be a dear man called Ken Monro, who had been a troop commander when we landed. This was eccentric — a considerable step down — but I greeted the idea with joy: I had been a "stooge", with no command of my own, for long enough. In future battles, instead of a hole in the ground, my habitat would be a room with a view (ideally some ruined attic). The nine OP officers, who swanned about in their little carriers in support of the infantry, quietly considered themselves to be the death-or-glory contingent. Of those who had landed in Normandy, five had been killed, the other four had got an M.C. "I wish I could tell you," I wrote, "the wonderful escape that was — real life again, with its dignity, its responsibility and the choices that make it interesting."

Operation "Veritable" followed. This was the assault into Germany, into the Siegfried Line, on a front of five divisions, with our own in the centre. This country between Maas and Rhine is heavily forested, and on the very day we started with the biggest barrage we had ever taken part in, the frost collapsed into a soaking, squelching thaw. The battle lasted for eighteen days, much of it within the sinister, interminable, heavily-mined Reichswald, crawling with Germans alive or dead. C's brother David, the little boy who had been such an obstacle at Hayling, was killed in this, his first battle, rising to his feet to lead his Grenadier platoon into action. Those who survived were lucky, not least I and those with me, considering my minimal experience of my new job.

> Can you imagine the joy of returning under the stars in one's little carrier, with one's little crew, battered and dirty but together, and demanding the best room in the farmhouse and cooking a luxurious meal and going to sleep? Put down on paper it sounds so simple. It needs setting to music.

Invading Germany brought new preoccupations. Paragraphs from different letters convey some of them:

> My personal resolution to be stern and ruthless with these people was rather shaken by the first German word I saw on a building, which *would* be the word "Konditorei"! Anyway I did have the satisfaction of symbolically tearing in half a repulsive book of anti-Jewish propaganda which I found among the ruins.

This non-fraternizing business is rather interesting. I had fully intended to be correct about it and to tell myself that a people is responsible for the crimes committed in its name. But in fact is it? I doubt it. And it's obvious that a great many Germans are genuinely glad to see us and are bitterly hurt when we refuse to look at them or speak to them. It's the last thing they expected. It may do no harm, it may be safest, but it's damn difficult. *I* can't apply it either to the very young or the very old and I can see the troops can't either.

We were ordered to evict all civilians from this area. I hated this, but next day found them all encamped in the forests nearby, obviously enjoying the picnic, with wild shrieks coming from the depths of the woods where their children were playing Red Indians.

Far worse is the subsequent vandalism (no other word). The Canadians are particularly bad. All the furniture is hurled out of the window, and the feather-beds and heavy sideboards of the house-proud Germans are either burnt or left to rot in the rain. Their store cupboards are then raided, their drawers searched for watches, fountain-pens or cameras and their pigs and poultry killed and eaten. A complete and sordid wilderness is left.

One reminds oneself all the time of Warsaw and Rotterdam and London and one tells oneself that this will teach them never to embark on war again. But the innocent suffer with the guilty — and will either ever rest until somehow, some day, they get their revenge?

Anyway, those who wanted their eye for an eye have got it. The homeless women push their prams through the rain; the priest goes into custody with the prisoners of war; the little homes are ground to powder. I only wish I didn't have to watch it.

I continued to be obsessed by this aspect of things

This prosperous and cosy countryside is a surprise. The people are nearly all glad to see us, as we represent the end of the war, and there is a real show of white flags in every village. They applauded the first troops into Osnabrück, which was awkward, and you feel that the children rather resent not being allowed to. There is of course a minority of high-principled and probably bereaved women who won't speak or look at us, which makes me unhappy — but the majority are, well, just the same as we knew them years ago and bitterly surprised by the curt and sometimes even brutal treatment they get. There's no doubt that Vansittart has won. The German people as a whole are being made to suffer — old people, women and children with the rest. The pretty girls get off lightest, as you'd expect. I think it is wrong. Most simple people can't be held responsible for war — they merely suffer from it.

The march from the Rhine to the Elbe was no triumphal progress. Ambushing our slow Churchills in a narrow lane at dusk was easy as pie and they burnt merrily: one such evening, stuck in a traffic block, I watched the two in front of me go up and it was plainly our turn next. More sophisticated harassment came from cobbled-together Panzer formations. Joining regimental HQ for a night's decent sleep in a remote townlet called Stadensen, not far from Belsen, which the Division had just uncovered (sharing a voluminous German duvet with the M.O.), we were woken at 3.30 a.m. by a column of tanks and other armoured vehicles. Broad American voices. They were in fact Tigers and a tremendous cannonade ensued. We extricated ourselves as best we could while the whole place went up in a grandiose conflagration. There were also the teenage guerrillas who called themselves Werewolves.

The other evening we caught a couple of Hitler Jugend. They said they just wanted a bed in the pub we were in but on being searched they had uniform under their clothes and were armed. We suspected they were the precursors of another raid so we subjected them one by one to some pretty terrifying cross-examination. We stood them in front of a table at which we sat, with various weapons on it. We shone a searchlight into their eyes while one of our German Jews (who interprets for us) shook his fist in their faces. We felt the most awful bullies. They were unbelievably brave. The youngest, who was only 14, answered all our questions in his treble voice without flinching, and though he was very frightened he did not break down. They were innocent, or they would have been liable to be shot.

The next night, by way of contrast, we spent in a circus. It was the only billet we could find. As we arrived the elephants were clumsily perching on their barrels, clowns tumbling, trapezists spinning in the air. Round the big cooking fire in the courtyard gathered afterwards the most fantastic crowd of freaks, animals, young men in sky-blue and gold, sham blondes, Russian D.P.s and maybe quite a few ex-German soldiers quickly changed into civilians.

And so, finally, it was spring. With April's soft airs came an unstoppable relaxation of everybody's inner tension. Barriers, principles, confrontations, hatreds built up over six years melted and came unstuck.

Yesterday was one of those fantastic days. We drove down miles of main German road, through a flattish country of woods and bright-green fields and orchards. The birches and poplars were misty with green, blossom just bursting, and everything growing almost visibly. The farms (now undamaged) already have a German charm, with bright shutters and painted beams, and the gardens are characteristically tidy — over tidy. But the point is that towards us came the most extraordinary procession you ever saw. It lasted all day, with intervals. It consisted, as far as one could see, of the whole of Europe, trekking westwards out of Germany, pushing handcarts. I suppose they were mostly freed prisoners of war, but there were a lot of civilian workers, Dutch, French etc., and a good many Germans. Weatherbeaten, rather square-headed men in viridian-green military coats turned out to be Russians. "Russki, russki, bravo," they shouted; "bravo!" we shouted back. There were a good many Italians, dark and dirty, smiling. "*Italiano? Va bene?*" I tried them with. "*Si, si, signor,*" they seemed to understand. As for the French, they of course were easily distinguishable as all their handcarts flew the tricolour and they also had it in their hats — incredible hats, top hats, chef's hats, berets. The French were the happiest and most crazily dressed of all. There were other nations less easy to identify, some very lame and tired, and sometimes a lonely old man in some unknown uniform shuffled past with a stick, mad and solitary, glaring at us. Some had horses and carts with girls on board, presumably German, wearing their friends' military greatcoats. A German soldier asked me to take him to the nearest place he could surrender, so I gave him a lift on my carrier; then we saw a German officer and some soldiers walking back down the road on their own, so I dropped him off. He was polite and absurdly friendly. So was the roadside population, which smiled and would have liked, one felt, to wave.

Altogether the war seemed suddenly to have gone haywire, to have become an artificial affair of governments and generals not taken really seriously by any of the peoples concerned. Here were all the peoples of Europe, hopelessly mixed up, quite indistinguishable, trudging along in the spring air, having at least one dominating thought in common — that the war is nearly over and they are damned glad. The war has become a farce — or is it the spring?

I felt then what I have so often felt — how much Europeans have in common — and wondered whether this fantastic mix-up and tangle that they are now in, quite beyond the power of authority to straighten out, might not make them realize it too. Must we laboriously put them all back in their little boxes?

At the end of the month we took part in our last assault crossing under surprisingly heavy dive-bomber attack — the Seine, the Rhine, and now the Elbe — and on the 1st of May, not without sadness, I packed up my stuff and joined Victor Balfour at 8 Corps as his unofficial A.D.C. It was a busy time for him, and mind-blowing for me. We drove through devastated Hamburg, a silent lunar landscape totally devoid of life. Not a cat moved in the rubble. It was obvious that Germany could never recover. We took the surrender of Lübeck and had calls from other towns all over the place, begging us to take them over before the Russians got to them. He sent me to pick up a senior German general, von Blumentritt, who was looking for someone suitable to surrender to. A smallish, rather Jewish-looking man, he put out a black-gloved hand, and I automatically took it, to my bitter regret afterwards. Later in Victor's office, as chief of staff of all the German armies in the north, he offered their surrender, but Victor was told that this must include Denmark and Norway. This he did not quite have authority for.

When it was all over I copied out for C some lines of Whitman's.

Word over all, beautiful as the sky,
Beautiful that war and all its deeds of carnage
        must in time be utterly destroyed,
That the hands of the sisters Death and Night incessantly
   softly wash again, and ever again, this soiled world.

Chapter six

DISASTER TIME

As a paid-up supporter of the Modern Movement in architecture
(i.e. a novice member of the MARS Group) I had been just in time to
meet some of the lions of the Movement in the 1930s. A dry Martini
with Chermayeff in his elegant apartment in Bayswater, a whisky
with Wells Coates in his high-tech studio in Yeoman's Row and, most
elevating of all, a lager with Lubetkin on the Friesian-cowskin settee in
the famous Highpoint One penthouse — it was like being elected to
the Royal Society in the days of Newton and Wren, or even a member
of the circle of Pico della Mirandola, so certain was I that I was in at the
birth — the difficult, delayed birth — of a new age. Of course there
were embarrassments. After dining with Paul and Brenda Willert in
their little house in Chelsea we were asked to give Gropius a lift home.
Glancing through the back window one should have seen his head
protruding from the "dicky" of the Renault. We stopped and got out.
We had forgotten it had no seat, and found him grovelling among
jacks and spanners on the steel floor. This was my only contact with
him, and with Le Corbusier I only had the magic of his writing, the
verve of his sketches and the strange unreality — almost as of the
artefacts of some extra-terrestrial culture — of the photographs of his
completed works. Most uplifting of all were the four nights in May
1939 when Frank Lloyd Wright delivered his personal "Declaration of
Independence" to a rapt student audience filling every gangway in the
lecture hall of the RIBA.

> I declare that the time is here for architecture to recognize its own
> nature, to recognize that it is out of life itself for life as it is now lived
> — a humane and therefore an intensely human thing . . . to be lived
> in and to be lived in happily. . . . It rejects all grandomania, every
> building that would stand in military fashion, heels together, eyes
> front, something on the right hand and something on the left. . . .
> Why then do you not trust life? Why does not great England on
> behalf of this great upward swing of life, on behalf of this desire to

serve and interpret and develop humanity with fresh integrity; why does England not trust life?

To which the only possible reply, in the circumstances, was *morituri te salutamus!*

Occasionally in the war years I was sent books for review in the *Architectural Review* by J. M. Richards, then its rather formidably left-wing assistant editor. He and I and all of us, as those years wore on, began to see modern architecture and "progressive" politics as inextricably interwoven. The words "social justice", which had not hitherto come my way, were given dramatic meaning for me by Dick Crossman in a splendid speech he delivered, perhaps to the Fabian Society, when I happened to be on leave in London, when for the first time he put forward the concept of a safety net through which no individual must be suffered to fall — later to be codified in the Beveridge Report. On the international plane we leafleted our friends on behalf of Federal Union, the institutional abolition of the Nation-State, a movement which bloomed, for some strange reason, during the Phony War, had its moment of triumph when Churchill proposed it to France *in extremis*, then wilted in the blitz. Given my past life, given my present circumstances, I was becoming an ideologue, and not a craftsman/builder, which every decent architect ought instinctively to be. Soon my only expertise in regard to buildings was how to blow them to pieces.

Meanwhile, at their safe wartime distance, politics fascinated me. Europe was a melting-pot out of which almost anything might be moulded. Exchanging drafts of peace treaties with my father, I proposed a return to the old provinces — Burgundy, Württemberg, Tuscany — as the building blocks for our United States of Europe. This must mean regionalism for us too — at that time a vogue word among planners. The Liberals were for it, being as usual more open to eccentric ideas than the other parties. They had also signed Sir William Beveridge, whom they (wrongly) saw as a great electoral asset. Some time during the long wait of 43/44 I heard that the moribund, old-fashioned South Oxfordshire Liberal Association were looking for a prospective candidate. I saw this as another way to stand up and be counted against all the attitudes that had so riled me as a soldier — a gesture, rather than a political career, and one that would only be meaningful for me in my home constituency, where I knew I could count on having a Tory opponent "well to the right of Genghis Khan". (It did not occur to me that a commitment, and not a gesture, was what electors with any sense would be looking for.) I naïvely imagined that the Labour Party would not be interested in South Oxon, or would make a United Front deal. Later, when a "khaki election" moved into the foreseeable future, I nearly pulled out when I discovered this was not so, since I knew there was precious little to choose between the Welfare-State platform of the two parties. But so fluid and unpredictable and pleasantly amateurish was the grassroots political scene that it seemed silly not to have a go, particularly since it would give me some weeks at home when the war ended.

When the war ended, 8 Corps established its headquarters at Plön in Schleswig-Holstein, a huge, handsome, modern *Schloss* built as a cadet school and overlooking a spacious and beautifully curvaceous lake embosomed in pine forest. Here Victor Balfour set me up behind a desk as some sort of PRO, and from here, being musical, we made frequent trips into devastated Hamburg, where we encouraged the opera to get on its feet again and represented the occupying forces at a series of symphony concerts. Here emerged Good Germans, as they were patronizingly called, pinched-looking, shabbily dressed, with their beautiful manners. Less good ones made themselves acceptable in army circles through mutual horror of the Russians, which became harder and harder to resist as news came through of what had happened in Warsaw and of the state of affairs in their Zone. Other ranks made friends with German girls, walking rather sedately side-by-side through the woods at Plön and sunbathing quietly on Frat Beach, as it was succinctly called, on the edge of the sparkling lake. Here I and other enthusiasts sailed the elegant mahogany Olympic dinghies we had found in the boathouse. The silence, the sudden end of all action, was at first paradisal, later boring. This was my first experience of that common modern occupation — manning a desk all day with nothing on it but a telephone that never rings.

The election campaign in South Oxon was a glorious if bizarre contrast. All the family rallied round, including all three sisters — Nancy newly returned from foreign parts. They worked like galley slaves on the secretarial side, while C lent glamour to my public meetings, one of them at Ipsden attended only by a horse. A certain professionalism was contributed by ex-Councillor Bayley, who had quarrelled with the local Labour Party and volunteered to be my agent. My two opponents were Sir Gifford Fox (C) and Mr Sydney Cook (Lab), and we had fun with a poster enjoining voters to

LET

BRETT

COOK

FOX

This seemed to me in the true Eatanswill tradition, but was considered the act of a cad by local Conservatives. Half a dozen meetings a day kept us on the move, and most of them, unlike Ipsden, were crowded and enthusiastic, even if neither I nor my audiences had much idea what we were talking about. Like all inexperienced candidates, continually surrounded by euphoric supporters, I felt certain I was going to win and could hardly believe it when the poll produced the predictable

FOX

COOK

BRETT

Nevertheless, ten thousand seemed quite a lot of people, and I saved my deposit.

We had a week off after polling day, and spent it at Portmeirion, then charmingly shabby and secluded. Clough Williams-Ellis had been among my Jones Club lecturers at Oxford, so greeted us as friends. He was full of post-war commissions, including plans for Littlehampton, recently bought by an American millionairess friend of his, Weston super Mare, which had visions of becoming a blown-up Portmeirion, and for Redditch in Worcestershire, for which he had been jointly commissioned with Patrick Abercrombie. How about my coming along as junior partner and general factotum, he recklessly proposed, heedless of my total inexperience: I could bring him up to date. So this was to be my eccentric ticket of entry into the Rebuilding of Britain.

Back at Plön, as the summer declined, boredom became an almost mystical experience. I dutifully subscribed to a correspondence course designed eventually to lead to a town-planning qualification. Obviously designed for school-leavers (I was thirty-two), it was so elementary, so old-fashioned, so unintelligent, that my mind revolted against yet another Square One. I would have to learn by doing.

Meanwhile Clough applied himself to establishing my indispensability as an expert on Post-War Reconstruction, but it was not until the end of November that he got me home.

We moved back, with the four boys, into the aesthetically embarrassing house in Loudoun Road which I had designed ten years before and which had survived the blitz without a crack, and Patrick Abercrombie let me have a room in his office in Welbeck Street. We were a scratch lot, united only in our affection, indeed our hero-worship, for him. His wife's death, coupled with the fame of his two great reports on London, had driven him to accept commissions all over the world.

I have in these last days written my report on Hong Kong, completed Edinburgh, done an extra-consultancy comment on Karachi and sent a message to the *Union Internationale des Architects* — and now if there's time I want to deal with Miss Chissell's book on Schumann.

He would breeze in unpredictably, a neat bundle of energy and humane enthusiasm, hand out intuitive notes and diagrams for the skilful team to flesh out, then buzz down to Aston Tirrold for a couple of nights with his beloved daughter Deborah, taking in a few CPRE inspections on the way. This flair for the quick sizing up of situations on the ground was the one gift I was to "inherit", in some small degree, from him.

Absolutely nothing came of my plans for those first three towns. "Dickie" Gillson, in despair at the building controls, sold Littlehampton; Redditch, equally frustrated, later got itself designated a New Town, with the consequent priorities and high-powered staff; and Weston had to settle to remain its windy, casual Victorian self, never big enough to fill the vast sandy bay over which the sea crept reluctantly at high tide. But not before we had put on a colourful pie-in-the-sky Exhibition featuring Norah Glover's entrancing sketches, which Clough persuaded Mr Silkin to open in person. "Plan boldly" had been his ministerial message in the days when Hugh Dalton was still "walking with Destiny" — so I did, and thought it most unfair when his only question on going round was "how much will it cost?". I hadn't the faintest idea.

★

The country was bankrupt, rationing was worse than in wartime and architecture in the old sense was banned. Far worse than any of that, war with Russia seemed more likely than not. Only seven months after our "liberation" of Europe my brother-in-law, Evelyn Shuckburgh, wrote gloomily from Prague, where he was *Chargé d'Affaires*:

> One is compelled by the magnitude and complexity of wickedness to close one's mind to whole departments of thought. Only those of the very strongest character and stamina can carry the burden of all they see and hear. . . . It is no use worrying about the atom bomb all the time or about the people who are to die of hunger in Europe this year. These are simply part of the immense background of anxiety and misery against which all 20th-century people move. It cannot, I think, be dissipated by frontal attack, but only (perhaps) on the individual plane, by resistance to dogmatism. Communism has degenerated into dogmatism in almost exactly the same way as Christianity when it was represented by the Counter-Reformation and the Inquisition. . . . Perhaps one could compare Fascism to the extreme forms of puritanism. These twin evils, exploited by the third evil, ambitious "great" men, can be seen grinning and leering at each other down the ladder of history, and mankind can be seen tearing himself desperately from the embrace of first the one and then the other.

This closing of the mind to the state of Europe, of England, or of some other beleaguered country, was to become a regular feature of people's lives after the war — necessary if work was to be got done, but apt to make it seem trivial, particularly mine, which apart from imaginary town plans consisted of helping friends, or friends' friends, to get minimal alterations done or licences for minimal dwellings. I was the equivalent of a struggling Health Service GP — not the brilliant surgeon I had imagined.

An immediate question was the future of Watlington. My father had not had a bad war, conducting a huge correspondence, holding the fort on his various committees, rushing about England accepting under-endowed country houses for the National Trust, as has been delightfully recorded by James Lees-Milne. But with their children long since out of the nest (Jinny was now a committed disciple of Rudolf Steiner and would soon disappear to Dornach for good; Nancy was in Prague with Evelyn, Pinkie commuting between London and Martyn Beckett's roots in the North Riding) the house, with its 25 bedrooms, was obviously out of scale with their reduced circumstances. While I was away, C and her sister and their children had shared half of it, while the other half accommodated a couple of dozen Land Army girls. Brambles had taken over the park, pigs, geese and poultry much of the garden. Now it was put on the market, but half-heartedly, as C longed to move back rather than bring up her (so far) four boys in depressed and dingy London, and my practice looked like outgrowing the room in Welbeck Street. The answer was suddenly obvious. If we could market the garden produce, update farm rents, move the office into Colonel Tilson's north-facing drawing-room and the Victorian dining-room beyond, and convert upstairs and outbuildings into flats, it would cost no more than living anywhere else. It turned out that we could fit in eight families including our own, which was as large as I wanted the outfit to be. I knew that to be able to offer a home as well as a job would be an attraction.

And so in the spring of '47, at the end of that bitter winter in an unheated office in sheepskin boots and mittens, we sold up our 'thirty-ish house with its Vitrolite bathroom and Gordon Russell furniture, its lever handles and Pepler rug, and it was back to bolection mouldings, Kent consoles and ancestors on the stairs. The place had got me back, after twelve years in which I had broken its spell. In no time the myriad problems of managing and manning the little territory had me trapped in that unbreakable love-hate relationship that has kept such places going for centuries. Within a year I heard that the Welwyn and Hatfield Development Corporation were to appoint a consultant architect/planner to prepare the master plan for Hatfield New Town and be responsible for its architecture. "Are you sure you know enough?" my mother nervously and properly enquired. That had to take care of itself: I applied for the job and got it. It was not, it appeared (though it should have been), insisted upon that the applicant should move into the town, which would have ruled me out.

The first thing was to set up an office in Hatfield and find a partner to run it. I telephoned the AA School and asked about the most promising recent graduates. Kenneth Boyd, the first I saw, I found immensely impressive — a born architect, as far as I could judge, ten years younger than me, sensible, reassuring, well-informed. Partnership is often compared with marriage as a high-risk undertaking, and this was a *mariage de convenance*. Ken was a realist: he did not share my vision of Watlington as a Wrightian architectural commune, clearing land, wielding axes, sharing produce. The traditional English stereotype of the country gentleman dabbling in architecture blotted out, I fear, such fantasies. A winter as lodger in a rather sunless dwelling was enough to put anyone off: he preferred to run the Hatfield office from London, where he rightly saw his future to lie. So the practice split itself into a Hatfield/London one run by him and a country one run by me — the latter having a charming but risky tendency to appeal to architectural dropouts, intellectuals and early-day hippies. I had come (perforce) to see the architectural GP as a useful member of society, and I never refused any job, however dim, though occasionally aesthetic incompatibility might lose me a client. We did upwards of 300 jobs in that first decade, in a great variety of size and type, shoe shops, monasteries, farm-houses, laboratories, country-house alterations, and while few were important, even fewer were an embarrassment. Occasionally, within the limits of the general stringency, one could still build a glamorous modern house, and share in the *joie de vivre*, the transformation of life, that such houses expressed and conferred.

But the start was slow. The shortages and the frightful state of the world at the end of the forties were a distraction. War had for so long been our natural habitat that we lived every day with the thought of slipping back into it. With Stalin on the rampage in eastern Europe, we and the Americans only had four weak divisions in Germany. So dependent were we on the atom bomb that my father, in his usual style, proposed we keep a single soldier as tripwire on the Elbe. Orthodox opinion could see no alternative to massive re-armament. My reading list for 1949 contained the following titles:

The Problem of Pain	*The Haunted House*
The Dry Salvages	*The Unquiet Grave*
God and Evil	*Why was I Killed?*
Splendours and Miseries	*Deaths and Entrances*
The Cruel Solstice	*Another World than this*

To snap out of this I would drive over to Hinton, where Nicholas and Olga Davenport, positive by nature, close to the Government, yet sensitive to all our preoccupations as artists, kept the flag of hope flying. We saw the new decade in playing paper games before a huge fire. When Olga fell seriously ill soon after, the sonnet I sent her was heavy with the prevailing imagery:

> Armed but with words, each with a breakable heart,
> We face the heavy regiments of fate,
> And while the rumble deepens in the grate
> Throw paper challenges into the fire . . .
> But for our comfort, in the darkest night
> Of the snow-flurried winter, you have escaped:
> One prisoner over the wire and into the light . . .

and so on.

Communal life at Watlington had its snags, and as the immediate housing shortage eased, our makeshift flats began to lose their attraction. Market gardening had not worked out — C tending to dissolve in tears when Henley greengrocers were contemptuous of her lettuces. And I became increasingly conscious as I became more rooted in the land that a house of the size it was had no future as a family home. So in 1955 we moved the survivors out into the converted stables and cottages, the office into converted farm buildings, the family, with Nanny and Nellie, remaining alone while two-thirds of the house, including what was left of the original Stonor lodge, and everything that had been added since the eighteenth century, was torn down around us. It was a dusty summer. My father characteristically made the whole operation possible by paying for the demolition of the Wellesley Wing he had himself built. The Duke of Wellington, as the architect had since become, was deeply offended or, equally characteristically, pretended to be. What emerged from the ruins was a plain man's Palladian villa of 1758, with fronts on all four sides, awash in space.

Meanwhile the London end of things prospered. I had become something of a pundit, addressing the stage army of the good all over the place and endlessly churning out improving pieces in the architectural press and in the Sundays, weeklies, monthlies etc. In 1951 I found myself appointed, perhaps as gadfly to sting the surviving neo-Georgians, to the Royal Fine Art Commission, generally the preserve of senior and respected figures. With all this buzzing about I felt the need of a partner to hold the fort in the cowshed and look after our Oxford clients. This was Peter Bosanquet, a friend of Ken's, who moved, with me, into the hayloft and into a little minimal dwelling I built for him and Mary at Christmas Common. Having agreed to Ken's desire to operate from London, we euphorically scoured the West End for premises, finally settling for an attic in Regent Street. From here, come summer, we had a cheerful view of the colourful lunch-hour life of the West End roofs, which few passers-by are aware of.

In those days it was a proud thing, as it is in all forward-looking countries, to be an architect, and to be a housing architect was best of all. Hatfield was the main preoccupation. As New Towns went, it was a baby — 26,000 population, half of which was already working at de Havillands. It was initially seen by the Development Corporation very much as an offshoot of Welwyn Garden City, and I was enjoined to seek the advice of Louis de Soissons, its distinguished neo-Georgian architect. This I was arrogantly determined not to do. Hemmed in by main roads and inter-war muddle, we lacked the space for the far-flung neighbourhoods of the other London New Towns. I became immersed in a fight to raise densities, taking Old Hatfield's cosy Church Street as model of the feeling we ought to aim at. I failed, of course. The suburban — indeed the rustic — dream held sway in that part of the world. Instead of Coronation Street, the names proposed by the local Council for our first streets were (inter alia) Thrush Dell, Foxglove Close, Honeysuckle Glen and The Pasture. And of course the regulations were sacrosanct — 70 feet between frontages — and to knock ten feet off that seemed quite an achievement. Later on, when there were cars lining every kerbside, I could see I had been barking up the wrong tree. But that struggle for "urbanity", as it was called, that trivial ten-foot victory, did pay off in the eyes that mattered to us. When in 1954 the *Architectural Review*, under the heading of "The Failure of the New Towns", launched its attack on "prairie planning" and I sprang to their defence, Jim Richards wrote to me that "we have always regarded your work at Hatfield as the one exception to the architectural shortcomings in the New Towns". In all controversies the Corporation Chairman, Mr Gosling, and its Vice-Chairman, Richard Reiss, a pioneer of the Garden City movement, took my part most generously. This did not endear me to their staff, to whom this blue-eyed boy swanning over from a country house in Oxfordshire was inevitably an irritant. At one of my weekly lunches with the

General Manager he said, without noticeable rancour, "You will be remembered for Hatfield when the rest of us are forgotten." He was to have an unexpected opportunity of ensuring that this was so — if not in the sense he had had in mind.

I became aware before long of my lack of sound training as a designer: "my" houses were not a patch on Ken's. This, if we were to make the best of our skills, relegated me to the role of non-playing captain, or rather captain with safe pair of hands and necessary flair for the strategy of the game, but no run-getter. Over the years I realized I was a better painter and even poet than architect. But architecture, with its long lead-times and unlimited liability, is the hardest of professions to move out of, once you are trapped in it at my level of responsibility. I was also aware of the frustration of the indispensable run-getters at not having the lion's share of the credit. If you naturally felt this frustration it took a very good man not to show it.

After "density", my other preoccupation in the early days at Hatfield was to devise ways of overcoming the shortage of bricks and timber by some form of light-and-dry prefabrication that would do for housing what Stirrat Johnson-Marshall and William Tatton-Brown, down the road at Hertford, were doing for schools. This was naïve. We could not command a County Council's economy of scale. And while Ken's elegant "X" houses, with concrete block party walls, low-pitched gabled asbestos roofs and cedar or glass panels front and back, rippling along the hillside, came out marvell-ously on quantity surveyors' estimates — the aim then was the £1,000 house — the builders, happier with traditional methods and all the restrictive practices that went with them, stubbornly priced them out of competition — an early example of what became known as the English Disease. We built a hundred or so, then had to revert to wet-and-heavy construction. The next move, I thought, could only be to make contact with one of the big national contractors who already had their proprietary systems of mass production and persuade them to modify their designs to meet our aesthetic require-ments. Our choice fell on the Wimpey "no-fines" concrete system, and to avoid the grim monotony of necessarily long terraces I proposed we curve them to and fro along the contours. Ken found a Swiss aluminium sheet that solved the roofing problem posed by the curves. Wimpeys' architects' department produced all the working

My parents

and my in-laws

My father-in-law, Ebenezer Pike, drawn by his wife, Olive Snell,
here seen in her wartime studio in the Shell House at Goodwood

Watlington – the
north side

1925

1935

1955, emerging
from the ruins

The Wimpey houses at Hatfield, 1956

Guildhall Square, Portsmouth, 1976

C   Martyn Beckett   Pinkie

Jinny   Evelyn Shuckburgh   Nancy

drawings and we seemed to have hit on a sensible redefinition of the architect/builder relationship which was, incidentally, realistic in view of the absurdly low fee (£10 a house on large contracts) allowed to architects by Whitehall. The price was right, so we built 383 of them, mixed with other types, on a sunny slope with a fine view to the south-west, and they looked good — miniature twentieth-century versions of Lansdown Crescent.

On the night of the 3rd of November 1957 a violent wind roared like an ocean through the woods at Watlington, and early next morning, with the sky full of leaves, the telephone rang. There had been a serious accident at Hatfield; a number of "C"-type houses had lost their roofs; casualties not yet known. I jumped into the MGA and it was a doom-laden hour's drive. There were in fact, miraculously, no casualties, but some 50 houses appeared to be damaged and sheets of aluminium roofing were draped over back gardens like the debris of an air crash. My least favourite Corporation officer had been put in charge of operations and was enjoying himself in a Disaster Room in an evacuated house, and the WVS were doing their stuff with coffee, caravans etc. in wartime style. I wandered lonely as a cloud, unwanted, then drove away.

There followed months of listening to the night wind in fear that more might blow, and the briefing of lawyers — in the Corporation's case the brilliant young Leslie Scarman, QC. Our insurers could not afford that level of representation. My old Chairman and Vice-Chairman had by then gone, and I never discovered why the Board decided on a Public Enquiry instead of pursuing architects and builders through the Courts in the usual way. This procedure, which ensured maximum publicity, was, as far as I know, never followed again in the hundreds, even thousands, of building failures that were to be a feature of the next two decades. Silly ladies, as a consequence, meeting me for the first time, still lead off with "Oh yes, weren't you once in trouble about roofs blowing off?". It is the only thing widely known about my architectural career. The fact that the working drawings were the contractors' was neither here nor there: we had passed them. Ken, whose office had run the job, had to endure minute cross-examination on the position, length and strength of every nail. When the official report was finally published we and Wimpeys were held equally liable — a fleabite to them, a sledgehammer blow to us. Architect friends wrote to commiserate ("there, but for the grace of

God, go I"). Among the most generous was Mr Cornner, the Corporation's Chief Engineer, with whom we had had so many arguments. I felt badly about the limelight thrown on Ken as an individual, so I wrote, with Peter Bosanquet, to *The Times* to associate ourselves with him. They gave me some obscure legalistic reason for refusing to publish the letter.

The last of our big housing projects was at Basildon New Town. By then the shortages had eased and we could do the best we were capable of. Close into the town centre, it was the snuggest and most urban thing we had done, with small courts and closed vistas, and I had a job to sell it to the Essex county planners. When it was finished Ken put it in for the Ministry's Regional Housing Award, which we had won with our first scheme at Hatfield. But no sooner was the announce-ment made than a *Daily Mirror* headline proclaimed "Prize Project Springs a Leak", or words to that effect. Housewives were up in arms. The Award was officially withdrawn. I was due before long to succeed Robert Matthew as President of the RIBA. He sent for me and in his charming avuncular manner told me that I was really too accident-prone for credibility: Donald Gibson would step into the breach until things quietened down. Not long after the damage was done we were wholly exonerated.

By then centrifugal forces had asserted themselves and our three-some had broken up. Ken took over the housing and London jobs and remained in the Regent Street attic, Peter set up in Oxford and I was blissfully on my own in the hayloft. The disasters then continued. Among the Hatfield jobs was a pub-cum-community-centre-cum-assembly-hall I had designed for an enlightened local brewer, McMullens of Hertford. This high-minded idea had emanated from Henry Morris, the fine old social democrat who had pioneered the Cambridgeshire Village Colleges. Now news came that rainwater was getting into its strawboard roof insulation, turning it to manure. Back to the insurers, but the advice they received, after a full investigation, was that the architect was in no way liable — it was a contractor's error, not a design fault. They would meet any claim (and it was a large one) only if the architect was found liable in the Courts. Another Hatfield drama, whatever its outcome, would make splendid newspaper copy and finish off my practice. So I went cap-in-hand to Edwin McAlpine, the chairman of the contracting firm, told him the story, and asked him to meet the claim, which he most decently did.

I was astonished, so punch-drunk was I, when in the midst of all this the Ministry of Works invited me to design the future High Commissioner's residence in soon-to-be-independent Nigeria. It seemed like a friendly gesture to give me another chance. I flew out in high spirits, landed at Lagos in a soaking, hot, November rainstorm, and spent some days exploring what was then an undeveloped and delightfully chaotic colonial capital. Future ministers charged about in a fleet of brand new Mercedes finished in the emerald and white of the future national flag. The new building was to replace (somewhat to my dismay) the nice old Edwardian Flagstaff House, with its white jalousies, on a wide lawn alongside the vast bay. Towering ships slid past, shaking the soft ground. In long talks with my hosts, Sir Ralph and Lady Grey, I learnt of the climate (let in the wind, shut out the sun), the life-style, the accommodation considered suitable for servants (shocking to me, but we would be unpopular with the Nigerian establishment if we bettered it). At dusk I would swim in the Government House pool next door, where the Governor-General, Sir James Robertson, was equally helpful. On my return I proposed — for it was only seven years since the Festival of Britain — that every item in my long creamy-white house, from the teaspoons to the carpets, should be the best that British designers could produce; Edward Bawden should design the Royal Arms, black mosaic on white, over the entrance, Reg Butler make the courtyard bronze, Jo Pattrick master-mind the interior. The Ministry, keen to turn over a new leaf, offered apparently unlimited resources; it was my first experience of sloppy Government financial control, and after the rigours of New Town housing it was a shock. It was also my first experience of the inability of British contracting firms to compete with the Italians in our own colonies. Nevertheless, everything proceeded prosperously. But in 1960 it was announced that the first High Commissioner would be Antony Head, a leading member of the Tory establishment and until recently Minister of Defence. Lady Dorothea was by no means the Colonial Service wife whose modest needs I had been briefed with. Her taste was Regency, and she had no wish to live in a sort of concrete Design Centre. Lord John Hope, Minister of Works in Macmillan's new Government, sent for me and in his friendly way said that my services were no longer required. A wing with a more adequate private drawing-room was to be added by his Ministry architects and the Pattrick furnishings — even the specially woven carpet —

scrapped. (Perhaps it was as smokescreen for this spending that the building was described by a Tory backbencher in the House of Commons as "a rather badly designed Corporation bath-house".) I asked for, and was granted, a last visit. This time I travelled Tourist, squeezed sleepless between an immense Nigerian and a portly German. Instead of Government House I was kindly put up by a PWD architect in mosquito-infested Ikoyi, and of course I had no say in what was happening to my building. Some years later I heard that the site had been bought up by the Nigerian Government and the house buried under a waterside motorway.

I flew home to a far worse disaster. My beloved C had fallen into an abyss of fear and desolation, which was to take her ten years and more of ups and downs, with the support of a trusted doctor, to understand and finally to transcend. I could not but feel that my own failings had been a contributory cause. We sent the four older boys (it was the summer holidays) to stalk stags in Sutherland with the Colonel, Olivia and Stephen to the seaside, and sadly, silently, side by side, we painted the attic windows — the only thing I could think of for her to do.

Chapter seven

THE WORLD TURNING

BROODING ON THESE things, I did not get very far. Schooled and conditioned for success, I knew I had a correspondingly over-developed sense of failure. But we had also been properly brought up to take the rough with the smooth, "treat those two impostors just the same" etc. etc., so we were strong on stoicism. Such useful lessons as could be drawn — take more trouble, take fewer risks — seemed to have been posted to the wrong person, cautious, in my case, by nature. If they were not, in the literal sense, disasters, if the fault lay not in my stars but in myself, if character is destiny (more old adages), where had mine gone wrong? I now believe that we should generally take "disasters" in all literalness as manifestations of a stumble in the rhythm that binds us to the universe. If we force the pace, treat time as an adversary, treat life as a race, run when we could walk, we trip up — sooner or later, often years later, often for years on end. We have lost touch, though we can regain it, with the stars in their courses.

The main advantage of living in England, it has been said, is that it is so handy for Europe. Convenient, yet dramatically separate. Those unclimbable cliffs I had patrolled in 1940 are potent symbols, possessed by no other nation. For centuries departing islanders have watched them recede into the mist with a variety of feelings — exhilaration, bitterness, relief, apprehension, escape — above all escape. Into those grey, disturbed waters, a slither on the map but a part of the main, we can dump the lot. Here we shed the claustrophobia, the complex relationships, the mean scale, the khaki landscape, the poor light.

Cyril Connolly's *The Unquiet Grave* did for us anti-heroes of 1944 what Robert Bridges' *The Spirit of Man* was designed to do for the legendary soldiers of 1914–18. Both wrote off the German world and glamorized the French, Connolly all the more affectingly from out of his *angst*, his wit, his sensuality, his dread of middle age. His was the France left out of our education. So, in 1947 we bought a Triumph Roadster, an eccentrically designed much-loved two-seater, which later developed dry rot in the dashboard, and in 1948 set off south, peeling off the kilometres to the tune of "Blue Skies", sizzling down the long black liquid reaches of Nationale Sept, the plane trees going sha-sha-sha through the open window, the windscreen yellowing with crushed midges, she with the Michelin beside me, a handkerchief binding her hair. . . .

Connolly was writing of before-the-war, but nothing had changed. We camped in the *maquis* of the Vaucluse, in the wild lavender above the Verdon, lived in a borrowed flat in St Tropez, just rebuilt after the American bombardment, where we were the only foreigners in the village and had the whole vast beach of Pampelonne to ourselves, wandered on to what was later to be the Costa Brava, where in the silent whitewashed port of Cadaques, in the only little hotel in town, we were the first English they had seen since the Civil War. The emerald water was unbelievably clear. The "grand object of travelling" could still plausibly be (as Johnson said) "to reach the shores of the Mediterranean", and there to submit to that other love-affair, with the landscape of ilex and olive, that was, with my love of the mountains, to pull me two ways for the rest of my life.

It still seemed possible we might have the federated Europe I so desperately wanted. "*On l'aura, l'Europe?*", some Provençal peasant asked me. How imaginative, I thought, how unlike the British! It was not till years later that Dominic de Grunne explained to me that the chap probably meant it in the sense of "*On les aura!*" — and was dead right. *Better done in France* was the title of a book of that time, and after years of confinement to British rations and British insularity this became (and remained) an obsession. It was the latest version of the old love-hate relationship. To begin with, the French resented being liberated — resented our having had all the luck. Later, the British resented their having all the skill. But at least it had not yet become an embarrassment to travel in a GB car that proclaimed us citizens of a country that was both curmudgeonly and incompetent.

Prosperously unaffected by the neuroses of convalescent Europe was my other country. I had not seen my Heckscher cousins for fifteen years, so in 1953 I wrote to Bunnie's husband Philip Hofer, the Houghton Librarian at Harvard, and asked if he could fix me some lectures on the New Towns, the only marketable subject I could offer. This he most energetically did, so that autumn we sailed in the *Queen Elizabeth*, so that C should come ashore in New York, one of the experiences now virtually lost to the traveller. She kept a diary of that time, written up in trains and planes and in the small hours after the marvellously generous hospitality such travellers were given.

24 Sept. L and I sailed for America this morning at 12.40 in the *Queen Elizabeth.* She towered majestically above everything at Southampton. Christopher and Michael came to see us off, and there they were as we sailed away, standing in a little knot of tiny people waving handkerchiefs, gallantly, waving and waving until they were too small to be seen and the pouring rain blotted them out. We left Cherbourg at dusk and saw the last friendly lights of France vanish on the far dark horizon, turned our heads towards the vast Atlantic, and went to bed.

25 Sept. One sits for hours beautifully wrapped up in a navy rug with a scarlet lining, gazing out at the enormous arc of sea and sky and the most beautiful green road left behind us over the waters. There is something so eternally soothing about those vast acres of water with the clouds lifting and falling upon their surface. One can read and dream and nothing (except hot soup at eleven) comes to disturb one's dreaming thoughts, or the speculations and absurd romances that one weaves round fellow passengers. To get enough exercise we jump over the barrier on the boat deck and damn well walk the 1st-class deck which they never use. Ten times up and down is a mile, and how exhilarating it is, pacing ahead down the smooth deck with the sea skimming and flying past, first into the wind, meeting it head-on and forcing oneself through it, and then about turn and back swimming with it.

26 Sept. We have been majestically riding a very strong south-westerly gale all day, great mountains of water come rolling towards the ship, lift the noble weight as if it was a toy, and leave her plunging down upon the strong smooth under-curve between the bosomy waves. The spray is snatched from their crests and flung away — very wonderful but oh! I feel so sick!

30 Sept. We were given a day in a million on which to enter New York harbour. We got up at 5.30 and watched through the pale glimmering mist, the first dim silhouette of the Statue of Liberty emerge into the fine, solid and inspiring figure that it is, and then, like magic, came gradually one by one the romantic towers and sky-scrapers of Manhattan; they were surrounded by a pinkish iridescent mist, and loomed out of it like a dream. Silently we got nearer, and more appeared, and then sounds, sounds of the land came over the water to us and smells of America. Then there were the cars, hundreds of them, one after the other, with the sun glinting on their roofs, pouring into the City as if they were on a conveyor belt; never ceasing, they came in an endless line. As we came nearer our dock, one could look down the streets to the sky the other end like long, jagged ravines.

The Hofers were on the dock, and that afternoon Bunnie drove us up to Cambridge through 250 unbroken miles of soft second-growth woodland; then, after a couple of nights in their deeply shaded 1830 house, on to their cottage in Maine.

2 Oct. We are on a hill looking over russet golden woods to the sea, stretched out blue and dotted with islands — purple mountains and cicadas singing, but above all the air; I shall never forget the feeling of freedom and happiness on simply breathing in this incredible air after the stuffiness of everywhere we've been so far. It is pure and clear and resinous and new life flows into one with it. The house is perfect, one big room, with an enormous fireplace, in which practically a whole birch tree burns, everything made of wood, and so wonderfully warm, the bedroom walls made of pine, plain and simple, and smelling the same clean resinous smell. Utter silence outside, no one for miles, only the cool, clear sky shining with stars and the tiny house, a haven of solace and warmth and complete peace. This morning is like champagne, hot sun and cool air; breakfast outside cooked in a minute on the most elegant stove, talk in the sun, with the incredible view of mountains, sea and islands spread out before us.

Up till now I've felt (since we landed) rather like a piece of the American bread, foolishly light and inconsequent, and still; with no feeling or vibration anywhere, kind of static; but here one has all the excitement and sense of adventure from the tremendous vigour and vitality and energy of the American people which they must get from these great stretches of land, so much that is wild and unbroken and full of promise.

Next day we lunched with Andrew Wyeth and his family of three generations on the rocky edge of the ocean.

3 Oct. Andy Wyeth is tall and slim (the slimmest jeans I've ever seen), he has long lean legs and a most individual and fascinating walk, a huge head with stiff hair and very expressive hands. He has a rugged quality, with great sensitiveness and believes that one should paint where one belongs, bringing to each object one paints the love, and knowledge one has of it. There was something moving and re-assuring about this family of people, who all understood the real true values and who believe in the things and people they love with a strength and faith that nothing and no one could shake. Their life is so free, because they make it so.

4 Oct. Another shining breakfast in the sun with a cool wind above us in the woods. We set out early with a rucksack full of cheese, bread and oranges, old shirts and "sneakers" to climb in. We had to put them in the car to change into later, as we were calling on some people called Dodge who live in a grand house and one had to be tidy. Nothing could have been more of a contrast to yesterday. The house, very lovely Regency, grey weather-boarding with the Captain's Walk on the roof, high slim elm trees in front, right up to the façade. A maid showed us in and then inside were three whitish-haired American ladies, one of whom was tall, distinguished-looking. Mrs Dodge, who was a Miss Henry (a very rich and aristocratic family of Philadelphia), married Donald Dodge, an enormous rough diamond of a man who I should think the Henrys hadn't approved of *at* all! He fell for this house where it *had* stood miles down the coast and was determined to bring it to its present beautiful site on the edge of the sea (which he had also fallen for). So on a barge the *entire* house was transported, chimneys and all! They thought that the barge would split open and sink once or twice during the perilous journey when the sea became rough, but all was well and there it is, wallpapers copied most beautifully from old ones, lovely furniture and, most fascinating of all, the most exquisite collection of glass of all colours — arranged in the windows so that with the light shining through they looked like stained glass. Everything in the house was in its place and the light was dim due to all the sun blinds being down, and one felt very little air penetrating in anywhere. One wouldn't have dared misplace a single object. Outside the garden was lovely, two borders going down to the incredible blue of the sea, and somehow it was a strange contrast, the beautiful, impeccably kept lawns and flowers leading to the wildness of the waves and rocks. It was all stuffily stultified and yet it had a dignity and beauty and I liked Mr Dodge, who loves his garden in a rough strong way, and to whom no journeying would be too far or too difficult, if at the end he was going to procure a lovelier lily.

We then escaped in our car, drove to the saddle between two mountains, changed our clothes and started on our climb. We walked through the forests first and then got out higher up on to great grey slabs of mossy rock which were lovely to walk on. The forest was full of golden light from the shining glory of the turning leaves — from crimson to bright ashy corn colour, with, always, the deep dark background of the evergreens. Like tall sentinels the slender pale-white birch stems stand out. And it was so strange to walk in woods that no one had ever tended; trees lived or died in their own time, and all around us where we ate our lunch lay the gleaming white bones of those that had fallen, while others were left standing straight, upright, stiff and dry. We lay in the sun for a long lovely time and then we came back for the last night before returning to Cambridge and Lionel's first lecture to-morrow.

5 Oct. We went to M.I.T. for Lionel's first lecture. It went very well indeed; he looked distinguished and spoke with authority, feeling and integrity and one was proud, watching these American faces being shown beautifully selected pictures of one's small brave country and the civilized and careful way we are trying to solve our planning and building problems. The Questions were great fun afterwards. Lionel is brilliant at answering and in no time the thing had become a most animated discussion. The general feeling was why don't we build enormous Corbusier buildings of glass and in fact be more daring and forget Traditions etc. L explained that the English don't want this, but you wouldn't expect students to be satisfied by that.

After another lecture, at Yale,

6 Oct.   Here we go, smoothly and comfortably in the express train "Mayflower", non-stop to New York. We are travelling the cheapest class, but in extremely comfortable seats beside enormous wide windows, from which one can see the whole countryside; the train moves over the lines easily, like silk, and one feels warm and happy.

From Grand Central Station we drove down Park Avenue to Augie's brownstone house in the East Nineties, where his French wife Claude, still un-Americanized, had an unregenerately French meal waiting.

8 Oct.   Lionel and I set out and walked along the wide pavements in the clear air and hot sun. There is a lovely width about the main streets which gives a feeling of well-being. The Lever Building is very exciting with its sheath of green glass, and walking about in the clear sunny air with the great skyscrapers towering above, one felt vividly alive and full of joy.

This was how she was; this was how America seemed, before the disasters of the sixties. Augie and I were both forty that year, but he seemed much more mature to me than I did to myself — he was already in demand as keynote speaker at architectural and planning conventions. He was intensely interested in my world, as I in his, and we shared the conviction that we knew what needed to be done. At a huge, rich dinner given by Mrs Reed, the proprietor of the *Herald Tribune* (on which he was a leader-writer), the old lady tapped a glass and ordered me to tell the assembled company exactly that — so high, she said, was England's reputation in my field. Another day, with his friend Ed Barnes, who was later to design their pinewood camp on a wooded islet in Mount Desert Bay, we drove down to Connecticut to see Philip Johnson and lunched euphorically in the famous glass house. The tall trees all around it streamed with the brilliant sunlight of the early fall, in which nothing seemed impossible.

High from lack of sleep, we caught a train to Washington D.C., where old friends, Jake and Ernestine Carter, put us up. My lecture was too pedestrian in theme for the Institute of Contemporary Arts, but was a smash hit at Howard University, then an exclusively black institution. Next day we blew all the lecture fees on air tickets to New Mexico.

Thirty years had passed since my Aunt Doll (Brett) drove out of the railhead at Santa Fe up the long rough road to the Spanish settlement of Taos on its high plateau, and twenty-three since D. H. Lawrence had died at Vence, but there in Taos his three women still lived. Mabel Dodge, the original discoverer of the place, very New England, very school-mistressy, gave a party for us at which her Indian husband, Tony Luhan, sat Buddha-like in a corner under a low flame-like lamp, responding with an occasional grunt to C's gallant attempts to converse, then stumped off to play patience in his bedroom. Frieda, with her Italian husband, gave a much jollier luncheon, chickens torn apart with bare hands, in her room lined with Lawrence's erotic nudes. She and Brett had moved down from the too cold, too numinous mountainside ranch where they had once had a flaming row about the disposal of Lawrence's ashes, and built themselves houses nearer the village — my aunt's adobe studio out in the desert sagebrush, treeless, sunbaked, on the edge of the Indian lands. The Esher arms in full colour emblazoned her garage doors; inside — an amiable slum, full of her paintings of secret Indian ceremonies. Every Indian we met spoke in praise of her, as she drove us wildly in her battered station-wagon all over the vast, radiant landscape. "Scream, Lionel, if you want me to stop!" At night, outside the snug mud-walled cottage she had borrowed for us, glittered more stars and galaxies than we had ever imagined.

And so we flew home. C's last entry reads:

> Flying east and home at 19,000 feet, leaving a blood-red sky behind and straining towards the first gleam of light ahead. How jolly nice the Americans are! Everyone is one's friend. I slept for a short time with the moon shining on my pillow, and when I woke, there below lay gathered garlands of light — lights of England's gentle, sleepy towns.

Three months after our first return from Taos, I was off on the lecture trail again. The British Council asked me to be British representative at an international housing and town-planning congress in Delhi and then to tour the cities of India, peddling the same subject. In freezing weather I took off in a noisy converted bomber, but after a couple of hours something was wrong and we turned back to Heathrow, then a couple of huts on the Bath Road. After dozing the night on wicker chairs in a corridor we were off again — 48 hours, with stops at Zurich, Rome, Cairo, Bahrein and Karachi. This made India seem a proper distance away.

One's first drive into Delhi out of an English February is a psychedelic experience. The crowds, a kaleidoscope instead of a grey gruel, weave their bright patterns on a backcloth of pale-beige, washed-out, rutted earth and dusty trees occupied by black birds of prey. Everything appears to be in ruins. Privilege is to live and work in a paradise garden behind a high wall.

I write in my high-ceilinged ground-floor room in the Cecil in Old Delhi — very British enclave, tennis going on outside, flowers of every season blooming, and the leaves, oddly enough, turning and falling in the warm evening sunlight.

Then straight off to a preliminary orange squash with other Congress delegates, flocks of green parakeets screaming across the afterglow sky. It is not always so pretty. On a later visit I arrived in the dark, the headlights picking out the huddled pavement sleepers that made it seem a city of the dead. Beauty and squalor, intelligence and ineffectiveness, vitality and disease: I was struck, all over India, by these oppositions — the door in the mud hovel opening to let out a beautiful girl in a dazzling sari, the corpses floating down the Jumna in the shadow of the Taj, the look of complicity and shared amusement in the eyes of a ragged Sherpa child, the huge apparatus of bureaucracy manoeuvring problems that are known to be insoluble. The Congress itself was a case in point — the high-pitched voices, the bad acoustics, the hopeless compromise resolutions. I shirked as much of it as I decently could, exploring with an English girl, in a mood of intense joy, the courts of Shah Jehan ("if there is happiness on the face of the earth, it is here, it is here, it is here") and wandering among the ruined tombs in the "campagna" to the south, then drinking late with cynical European journalists or pioneer American dropouts: the relationships of people who will never meet again have a vividness of their own.

After a week in the capital, I set out on my travels. Here are some sample days.

10 Feb. Interesting day. Flew off to Lucknow at dawn, to be met at the airport at 9.30 by a formidable delegation. We then toured the town. It is unexpectedly attractive, with crumbly yellow and red stucco streets and lots of lawn and trees.

Lunched very grandly with the Governor of the United Provinces, Sentries, A.D.C., and through a series of under-secretaries to the innermost hideous reception room in a cool, shuttered, stultified Victorian mansion that reminded me of Grandpa Heckscher's taste. Orange squash and a gold-embossed sheet telling one's place at luncheon — which was fairly heavy going, H.E. (a charming, intelligent, oldish man in a dhoti) doing all the talking, his wife occasionally putting in a pretty relevant point. Nobody else spoke.

It dawned on me that they had been given to understand I was a major figure in British politics. I was given tea by the Minister for Local Government, just he and I on his suburban lawn. A tiresome man who kept interrupting me to fuss about the table-cloth or mutter unnecessary instructions to the servants. And an odd tea: a cream bun, then hot peas in olive oil, then slices of potato in yoghurt, then salted nuts, then a guava.

On to my lecture to a terrific audience, all the Cabinet, and the Prime Minister in the Chair. As this lecture was only meant for small groups of professional planners I fear it was both above the heads of the large lay audience of 300 and beneath the dignity of the occasion. The dear old P.M. gave us a long fireside chat at the end, very sound stuff. It was quite a relief to dine with a dozen local architects in a vast empty room, though even this was hard work as I had to initiate every topic. Early to bed at the Carlton, a down-at-heel Alhambra among eucalyptus trees.

11 Feb.   Motored out, with escorts, into the country to look first at an agricultural training centre, white huts under ilex trees, then to inspect in great detail a "typical" mud village. It was surprisingly pleasant, not smelly (perhaps chosen for this). All houses have a walled court, and the better ones have rooms all round it. Women scuttle like rabbits if one appears unexpectedly. The headman's home quite elaborately moulded in mud — columns, niches etc., and brightly distempered inside, with thick elm doors studded with brass and painted clay dolls for the children. The only furniture large woven-string beds. Every object in the village is produced within it. Doe-eyed cattle and baby calves all about but no chickens.

Rushed back to lecture before lunch to a crowd of economics and sociology students at Lucknow University. A stifling hot lecture room. No questions asked, but unaccountable gales of laughter when I showed a block of flats for single people and young-marrieds.

After lunch, feeling pretty tired, we motored across the dead-flat, bosky, not un-English plain to Cawnpore. The combination of aggressive Indian driving and high-pitched Indian conversation unrestful, but eventually to my relief the horn gave out. We crossed the enormous Ganges. In Cawnpore, a chaotic mill-town now grown to a million inhabitants, we looked at red-brick industrial housing — pretty grim cell-like dwellings (one room per enormous family) with barred windows — then took tea with the local chief administrator and his good-looking, not excessively mousy wife. The ensuing lecture was a bit of a farce owing to electrical breakdowns, but I was told the audience was a distinguished one. After a whisky with the local British tycoon, nice old Scot called Sir E. Soutar, we drove home under the moon, chewing betel-nut.

How responsible are we spoilt Anglo-Saxons, with our incredibly high standards, for the poverty of the rest of the world? Do we now wash our hands of India? I suspect not. It seems that unless we take responsibility our civilization will go down in famine and war.

16 Feb. Calcutta. I write from the loneliness of an air-conditioned room in a de luxe hotel in a great city. Neon lights flash on and off and up and down the pavement pass endless young men in their shirt-tails and pyjama trousers. Occasionally a couple of middle-class Englishwomen in awful summer frocks.

In the evening a street battle developed all around my hotel. I saw it building up at sunset, with Communist agitators all over the Maidan whipping up excited groups. Later it became an affair of burning buses and trams, tear gas, stoning of the Police, a certain amount of shooting, and a lot of broken glass. We were all besieged in the hotel for a couple of hours while the battle raged outside. Eventually Gerrard and I got out and made our way with streaming eyes through pitch-dark streets (the lamps had been shot) full of nose-blowing people and littered with brickbats and broken glass. The only light came from merrily burning vehicles. Quite like old times. No taxis, but we found a rickshaw and visited a rather gay dance pavilion where we squatted on the floor amid a large, rather subdued crowd and watched an interminable series of unintelligible recitations, cacophonous music and clumsy dancing. Local colour. We escaped to his flat via back streets and had a bottle of Château Lafitte which he had got with great difficulty.

17 Feb. I drove out of town with Bandopadhyaya, its Chief Engineer, to look at Kalyani, which had been advertised to me as Calcutta's New Town. But really the trip had been laid on by B so that he might have me to himself in his car for three hours. He made the best of it. But I liked him and responded to his humane and rational quick intelligence. We drove through a richly tropical landscape of palms, bananas, mangoes and ricefields with some-times a bright-red Flame of the Forest, to Kalyani, some 35 miles out. It consisted of nothing but a bulldozed desert, a very bad Union Jack pattern of roads and a small number of third-rate buildings. But we talked about everything, England and India and birth control and religion and politics. On the way back I had an interview with S. K. Dey, head of the Community Projects Administration for Bengal, a clever official who made me see that there was sound *economic* reason for their neglect of Calcutta and Kalyani and their present concentration on regional development. One is struck by the youth of most of the people running India.

My lecture to Calcutta Corporation Officials was in the incred-ibly dingy Town Hall, a glorious shambles — nothing laid on, standing room only, deafening traffic outside. But I liked the voluminous Mayor and he seemed competent. Of course nothing looks like being done in my lifetime to clean up this derelict city, with its dirt and touts and unemployed, its bug-ridden families camping all along the pavements outside Government House. Whether they will ever succeed (as S. K. Dey put it) in "holding the line" here looks doubtful.

18 Feb. Driving for the last time this morning, as the sun rose, along the scruffy route to the airport, one saw the army of pavement dwellers like corpses in every attitude of abandon, swaddled in dirty blankets, or stretching or cleaning their teeth. Lorryloads of armed soldiers patrolled, or hung about at street corners. The excuse for this week's riots may have been trivial, but in the grey dawn their cause is clear — and just. With its impossible situation and weak, well-meaning liberal Government, Calcutta looks all set for Communism.

21 Feb. Up again and away before dawn. Landing at Hyderabad, I was embarrassed to find on the airport the ubiquitous Jean Canaux (a rival attraction, also lecturing on architecture), to whom I had taken a perhaps unreasoned dislike at the Delhi Conference. We have since been cutting each other dead all over India, but now we've had it, as we are to spend these two days together without possibility of escape.

Cheery little Fayazuddin, President of the Indian planners, met us both plus Canaux's large, silent travelling companion, and the next thing we knew we were all three to share a bedroom. At this I struck, and eventually found myself a guest on the top floor of a terrific modernistic villa, perched on a boulder-strewn hilltop overlooking the whole city. It belongs to a tall and handsome Moslem barrister, and for sheer dumb ugliness its interior (Cunard-liner-style) would have taken some beating. No sign of the rest of his family, indeed no sign of human occupation of the house at all, until taking photographs in the garden I ran into a bevy of little girls in white satin trousers, who screamed with fright. But then so would Olivia★ if she suddenly met an Indian in the rose garden.

One has the feeling that there is an enormous family in the house, but they hide with ingenuity and all I see is one of those overzealous Indian servants who almost lift the coffee cup to one's mouth.

Hyderabad lies in a savage volcanic landscape like Gethsemane by Mantegna, with monstrous round boulders casually perched on one another. It spreads for miles, but the old city is well defined by walls and gates and is laid out Roman style, with central cross-roads marked by a rather ugly stucco Arc de Triomphe.

It is remarkable as the only city I've seen of a million people with no motor traffic — nothing but bicycles and rickshaws at its centre. Plainer, nicer arches span each of the four main streets and produce intriguing perspectives. We padded about a large plain stone mosque in the evening sunlight, while worshippers prostrated themselves and flocks of pigeons clapped.

As usual, no blackout for my slides, and I had to talk the daylight

★Our only daugher, aged six.

out until it was dark enough for them to be visible.

We were taken to dinner in an even uglier house, this time in a dingy 1890 way, with palms in pots and facetious inscriptions carved on little slabs all over the garden. The garden seemed to be a monster rockery, with waterfalls but no water, and there, a score or so of men only, we rather lugubriously forked at a lot of spicy dishes in blinding fluorescent light which entirely destroyed the moon and the breathless beauty of the night. I talked to a depressed, neurotic Moslem architect who has never forgotten the massacres of 1947, resents the gross favouritism of the new Hindu politicians and sighs for the good old British days. Hyderabad is the only sizeable Moslem city left in India, and in 1947 the Nizam made a bid for independence. Patel's troops marched in and (one is told) massacred 400,000 men women and children and stuffed them down the wells.

22 Feb. We spent most of this morning in the Salar Jung museum — the vast, inestimably valuable collection of a crazy jackdaw billionaire who died here quite lately. It is nothing less than a bid to collect in one sprawling palace the arts and crafts of the whole world: thus — Louis XVI furniture (e.g. Marie Antoinette's dressing table), gilded Egyptian (Tutankhamun's Throne), brown English, horrible black Japanese, South Indian Bronzes, Wedgwood, Sèvres and Dresden in fantastic profusion, a thousand jewelled Moghul swords and daggers stiff with diamonds, Victorian white-marble sculpture, Pre-Raphaelite painting, medieval ivories, priceless Persian carpets, Indian and Japanese silks, miles of armour, yards of jade and crystal, Chinese dragons, landscapes in marble, carpets of woven ivory, unique collections of walking sticks, toy soldiers, snuff-boxes, clocks, dolls' houses. Emerging from this surrealist nightmare, though there were lots of individually lovely things, one was left with a sense of despair at the misplaced ingenuity and patient, myopic, ill-rewarded industry of the human race. Thank God, one felt, for the disappearance of the craftsman.

We were entertained to dinner — forks again, fried things and water — at the best club in town. It was rather like the Liberal Club in Henley. For an hour before dinner we sat round in a large circle, conversation desultory, while guests arrived at wide intervals. For the most distinguished we rose to our feet and he gravely shook hands all round the circle.

23 Feb.   Nice Fayazuddin, who spends two hours at prayer before breakfast, took me out into the country and we spent all morning wandering among dead cities, ruined tombs and unlikely-looking rock formations. We called at a charming, rather Spanish country house among mango groves and brilliant cannas, and were given a cup of coffee by the modest daughter of the house. She had a magnificent white horse from Arabia which followed and obeyed her like a dog. Tigers and bears shot close by festooned the walls.

27 Feb.   Bombay. Motored out to the Tata Institute of Social Science, in the suburbs, where I was to "lead a discussion" on the social aspects of housing etc. In fact they expected a lecture and had no idea of how to run a discussion; with the Director in the Chair the students were much too awed to open their mouths. A few cynical remarks came from one or two of the staff and I felt I had made no contact and only stimulated the defeatist element. One was depressed by their authoritarian yet at the same time imprecise teaching methods.

Tiny Ram Singh in a monstrous Buick picked me up in the afternoon to show me "some good architecture". The first thing I saw was some mad millionaire's junk-house and unbelievable technicolor rockery, then a lot of Ram Singh's mediocre blocks of luxury flats. The rare good buildings we flashed past were dismissed as "American". To his club, the MCC of India, in purple dusk, but the only drink he could offer (on account of Prohibition) was coconut milk.

1 March.   I was driven out of town to see "the Master Plan for Greater Bombay". But when I reached the seedy flyblown planners' office it could not be found. I was shown terrible bits of estate layout (concrete roads 30' wide right up to one's front gate) and the reasons why nothing intelligible is being done about Bombay were explained to me. Then back through miles of slums, where huge families each have one filthy tenement room for every human purpose, wondering at what point the vicious circle of Indian architecture and planning is to be broken. The answer one is universally given is "Nehru", which gives some idea of the trouble.

And yet, as I travelled up to Ahmedabad on the night train, a man stepped into my air-conditioned cabin who made me wonder if I had got India quite wrong. He was a tall, handsome, bearded man with an expression of extraordinary nobility and gentleness, who introduced himself as Gautam Sarabhai. Apart from listing for me the best ancient and modern buildings in Ahmedabad, he pretty soon made it obvious, but in the most charming way, that he was rather more knowledgeable and sensitive about modern architecture and design than I. He left me feeling how easy it is for the European here, and particularly the diarist, to make snap judgements about India and even be fool enough to announce them to Indians. I asked for trouble, but the interesting thing was the gentle and thus all the more devastating way in which I got it. I discovered afterwards that he is an industrialist, mainly cotton, and one of the richest young men in India. I met his brother later who is a brilliant (is there such a thing as a stupid?) physicist, married to a dancer. One of his sisters is Nehru's secretary, another is an architect who trained with Frank Lloyd Wright.

3 March. Baroda. Toured the town with a vanful of notables. Baroda is basically a tightly planned Roman-square, with central feature and arched approaches like Hyderabad, to which benevolent Victorian maharajahs added bosky parks and avenues, zoo, bandstands, and technical institutes. Independence eliminated the princely family, who now live in more than Irish decay in one of their three palaces, the vast gardens reverted to jungle and full of monkeys and jackals. As Ahmedabad goes up, Baroda goes plainly down, and I doubt whether its new status as University City can save it. The University is adding dumb red functional buildings, but its academic level is as low as usual.

All-India-Radio telephoned for a broadcast, so after lunch I recorded an unscripted talk at their local studios. It was typically free and easy. I found myself having to act as my own "producer". The young interviewer was very nervous, and so displeased with his own performance that it was difficult to stop him re-recording the whole thing. My voice, played back, sounded as awful as ever.

After that, in a temperature of 101 in the shade, I lectured to the students and officials in a blacked-out hall. At the end of a long bout of questions, I was to my astonishment formally garlanded with a heavy wreath of wet flowers, and a large Victorian posy was placed in my hand.

It is Siva's spring festival, and on the way home I stopped at a beflagged temple and watched all the women and girls of the town go by in their prettiest saris.

4–5–6 March.   My last two days in Bombay were an anti-climax. I addressed two more meetings. The first was at Bombay University — economics and sociology students, mainly women. Two voluminous nuns put me off by taking continuous notes of my entirely impromptu talk. The other meeting was the local Arts Club. Shouting down passing trains, I talked about painting in England, and there was quite a good argument on the familiar topic of How Artists are to Live, but confined unfortunately to three or four Germans. The Indians were silent. Here, it isn't just artists.

I was taken to see the famous Aarey Milk Colony, a model dairy farm where 15,000 buffaloes and their owners, formerly tenants of the streets of Bombay, now live side by side in a wild tract of rock and date-palms 20 miles inland. I had to brush up my A.I., milk yields etc., and to drink a pint of the finished product through a straw, while talking to the Danish manager, who spoke almost no English, on a high terrace surveying his whole domain. Unfortunately I don't like milk and can feel no affection for the water-buffalo, with her greasy hide and hangdog expression. However it is clearly an excellent and highly successful project, with all the latest hygienic equipment, and needs imitating all over South-East Asia. Rows of women were cutting the grass with scissors and removing each plantain by hand over great terraces of lush green lawn edged by row on row of brilliant flowers. Their homes, nearby, were 4-foot-high kennels of mud and reed.

My last date was to meet a few enthusiasts at the Town and Country Planning Association. Hodgson (an admirable British Council type) and I felt our way up an incredibly sinister staircase, flight on flight, dark, worn, wrapped around an ancient iron lift. Pure Dostoevsky. One stumbled over dustbins, expected corpses. Emerging into daylight at the top, we entered a shabby office full of dust and a sudden gale from nowhere. An old gentleman greeted us and we talked generalities until two or three others had stumbled in.

Then some "town-planning" drawings were produced, terrible things, office-boy stuff. At once a terrific argument about them flared up between two of my hosts. Both shouted at once, the gale rattled the windows, we all held down the hopeless drawings. Impossible to get a word in. After 15 minutes of this Hodgson and I looked at each other. There was nothing for it but to take our leave.

We walked home along the beach as the sun, a flattened balloon, slid down behind a black sea. The whole town is out on the beach at this hour, strolling or sitting in family groups, but not bathing of course, or making love.

That setting sun, at the same hour next day, lit up the whole of the Alps in the most spectacular panorama I have ever seen. In its warm afternoon we had flown the whole blue length of the Italian coast from Calabria to Portofino: the most lovable coast in the world. We had looked down on Crete, and seen the snows of the Peloponnese shining on the horizon. This was home.

India was still, on that visit, obsessed with the British, who were still to be seen in substantial numbers. Rejection symptoms were apparent: even the future official use of English was in debate. Architectural colleagues were on the watch for any tendency on my part to patronize, talk down, know all the answers, and in their impulsive way expressed their delight (and surprise) when they found that I did not (though I now see that my diary did). Having experienced these transitions it was interesting, the following winter, to see the Empire still in full swing in Africa.

Years ago, after a week firing our guns on Trawsfynydd ranges, I had taken a day off for a circuit of Snowdon. There was not a soul on the mountain, and I fell asleep in the warm sunshine on the crest of Lliwedd. After a time the scrape of boot-nails on rock woke me, and a handsome bearded climber appeared. He was Robert Donington, musician, whose wife Helen, it transpired, had been at Oxford in my day. We became friends and in due course they asked me to godfather one of their twin girls. But later they parted, and Helen married Andrew Cohen, a brilliant, unorthodox Colonial official with a special interest in Africa. He was now, in 1954, Governor of Uganda and we decided, by way of convalescence from some winter illness, to go out there for ten days. We were to join them "on safari" in the

remote south-west of the country, and as it lies exactly on the equator
we imagined heat and insects and took sun gear and bush shirts. In fact
we joined a motorcade of limousines in cool, showery grazing
country rather like the Cheviots. At cocktail parties for local officials,
ladies wore hats and long gloves. Underdressed both literally and
metaphorically, we had to borrow.

Still, it was Africa. We dined in thatched bamboo pavilions
superbly carpentered for the occasion, behind high leopard-proof
stockades. Afterwards, the stamp of firelit male dancers shook the
ground. We progressed south by coral-pink tracks into the country of
the elegant, snobbish Watussi and their stocky subject people, the
Hutu. Assembled in hillside Rubazas, or tribal assemblies, would be
entire rural communities, the sea of black heads shining in the sun as
far as the eye could reach. Standing on a floor of neatly combed hay,
the Governor would present portraits of our young Queen, then stride
off across the landscape, followed by the laughing throng. The
shepherds were colourfully cloaked, but the teenage girls, drawn up in
rows on the roadside, looked hopeless in their shapeless school frocks
or Girl Guide uniforms. We crossed misty lakes like Derwentwater in
ancient launches, to be met on the far side by a new District
Commissioner and his staff— splendid chaps all, decent, fond of their
people, whom we watched dispensing justice. Through intermittent
downpours we climbed higher and higher in gorilla-haunted bamboo
forest, to spend a night in the modernistic mountain-top home of a
Cypriot mine-owner and his forlorn Greek wife, in a land of extinct
volcanoes as high as the Alps.

In this remote region the tribes had no use for the up-and-coming
semi-urbanized Baganda who aspired to dominate the whole country.
On those rare occasions when we were alone with the Cohens,
Andrew sat silent at meals, or out-strode us across the green ridges,
brooding over his row with the Kabaka, the attractive, Sandhurst-
trained but wayward King of that tribe, whom he had lately exiled. As
a liberal intellectual, such a *coup* was against his nature, and he dreaded
its consequences on his return to Entebbe. It was also, as he well knew,
against the tide of history. The future of Africa lay with arbitrary
rulers like "King Freddie", and not with the parliamentary institutions that Andrew and his predecessors had striven so hard to
foster.

★

The years passed, and in the spring of 1958, convalescent from the Hatfield Enquiry, I had a message from Clough Williams-Ellis. His mother-in-law, Lady Strachey (whom we remembered reading to three-year-old Olivia after she nearly drowned at Portmeirion), had lately died and left Amabel a small legacy, with which they proposed to charter a yacht in the western Mediterranean. *Oronsay*, an elegant if elderly 60-foot schooner, complete with British "navigator", lay at Monte Carlo. Would C and I join as crew? They had already engaged a biologist they knew, and needed three more, so I recommended Liz Beazley, a handy girl lately in my office. This was a breath of air I needed. So on a windless afternoon, with a light swell, we all lay on deck as we headed south for Corsica, feeling rather sick. Amabel, an experienced yachtswoman and a splendidly experienced person, took the midnight watch, and I stumbled up from below at two to relieve her. The scent of the invisible *maquis*, still 50 miles away, filled the light airs from the south. South? A glance at the compass showed that we were pointed due north. Even now, I am not sure I should tell this story. We tied up at Calvi at dawn, with only the bakers busy in the alleys. Later we swam across the bay and wandered up valleys deep in aromatic shiny-leaved forest and overhung by fantastic rock peaks like a Magnasco. Later, when I came to work in the island, wild and grand though it was, I never saw such Baroque profusion.

The halcyon weather continued. In breezes we sailed, in calms we motored, our landfalls generally at sunset in small ports designed for craft of our size. It was the hour of the *passagiata*, and the buzz of talk came out to us over the harbour water. A small crowd would gather to watch us tie up, to whom we showed off our increasing expertise. Our last port before home was Portofino, and we reckoned to make Monte Carlo next day. It dawned bright and gusty, though it was hard to tell in that deeply ensconced harbour. Weather forecast was stormy, so we took a couple of reefs in the mainsail and foresail and slipped out into the westerly breeze, taking long reaches seaward and landward. Out in the Gulf of Genoa the wind grew into a Force 8 gale, the sun paled and vanished. *Oronsay* now scudded along excitingly, increasingly hard to hold, increasingly losing way westward as I had to ease her up. Around noon our navigator came up from below. He shouted we would never make it, had best down mainsail and foresail and run back east under a staysail for the nearest port. So we set about it. While I held her into the wind the sail crew tied themselves on with lifelines,

Clough vaguely to a Calor gas cylinder standing loose on deck. Impossible now to communicate except by signs, the wind tearing the top off the sea and streaming it across us. "What mad thing am I doing," C asked herself, "abandoning my six children?" But finally the struggle ceased and we joyfully turned and ran. We ran for three hours, myself at the wheel. Best not to glance over one's shoulder, where seas that seemed as high as the South Downs pursued us. Clough doggedly read a paperback in the lee of the deckhouse, Amabel at intervals conjured soup out of the swaying galley. Then the coaling port of Savona loomed up through the wrack, the seas crashing on the breakwater. The entrance (which we should not have attempted) was horribly narrow, but we shot through it, with Liz signalling from the prow and anxious faces envying my concentration. Silence, except for a distant roar. We glided in along the waterlines of immense cargo ships, their crews raising a cheer from high above us. We tied up as usual, then walked the warm afternoon streets crowded with shoppers. We walked on air, the most privileged people in town, possessors of a secret we could not tell them.★

So that year, my forty-fifth, was the year of the wind which, having blown my architectural career to pieces, gave me back my life. The year after, it was the whole world. In 1957 Jim Richards, concerned at the deplorable standard of British university architecture, had asked me to collaborate with Nikolaus Pevsner on a couple of articles on the subject (which drew a letter of protest from five knighted architects at this "disloyalty to the profession" — an illustration of the pitfalls of architectural criticism). It must have been that critique which suggested to the British Council an "advisory" tour of the Australian universities, which were up against the same growth problems as our own. A week in each city would make an eight-week tour. The invitation came at a time when I felt a need for solitude and self-examination, so in mellow October sunlight I set out from Watlington and flew west. Within half an hour of my taxi arriving in heavy heat at East 94th Street the whole Heckscher clan arrived for dinner (1 a.m. my time). Next day (I had been too tired to sleep), after the usual architectural runaround,. Augie had laid on a planners' lunch for me to talk to, then I was off overnight to San Francisco, still a bland, pink and white "Mediterranean" city that had not yet become the capital of

★Clough Williams-Ellis gives his own account of this voyage in *Around the World in Ninety Years* (1978).

the New Left and the Drug Culture. After a night with a young architect friend of Augie's I took off again at midnight for Sydney. We put down in the small hours in Honolulu, to be perfunctorily garlanded with flowers, then flew on into the dawn. Around noon, in intense heat and glare, we dropped down on to a tiny coral atoll roughly where the equator and the international date line intersect; seven hours later it was golden afternoon in lush, intensely green Fiji. It is the longest day you can have on this planet, even longer in this case because we were late into Sydney, with only an hour to change into white tie and decorations for the Australian Institute's Annual Dinner. Sydney was still a casual, slapdash Victorian city, with no skyscrapers, and my hotel was a shabby old place in Charing Cross, Sydney's Leicester Square, with traffic roaring and neon signs flashing all night outside my window.

After San Francisco Sydney seemed an immense suburb in search of a city, its Harbour Bridge, a stodgy British design, inelegant after the Golden Gate. A few grandiose Victorian commercial buildings, blighted, no doubt, by impending redevelopment, looked dingy in the brilliant light, which transformed a touchingly British procession — Salvation Army, firemen, Red Cross and St John's, Scouts, Guides, Brownies — into something almost surrealist — or so it seemed: I was still light-headed from lack of sleep, and next day collapsed with some painful internal obstruction and a high fever. I knew not a soul in Sydney, but the British Council representative, himself newly arrived, found me an intelligent new-Australian doctor. The claustrophobia in my gloomy room was the worst of it. The Council got poor value out of me in Sydney, which I saw through jaundiced eyes, and as soon as I was well enough I flew up to my next assignment, Brisbane, to recuperate. That nice place basked in the semi-tropical spring, and I stayed in one of those quiet verandah-draped provincial hotels, surrounded by jacarandas in full bloom, that have now, I suppose, disappeared from Australia. Wooden matchbox houses perched on slopes and the rather grand neo-classic public buildings were newly cleaned and floodlit. My sessions in the hilltop University went with a swing, and in between them (for I had been given far more time than they knew how to fill) I started on a book and strolled in the palm-studded park outside the door. Two or three spare days were spent on a long drive across the coast range into the ranch country of

the Darling Downs, and on a marvellous hike in the rain-forests south
of the city, with only the chatter of flamboyantly-coloured parrots
breaking the primordial silence. A Pacific swim in honky-tonk
Surfers' Paradise followed by a T-bone steak provided appropriate
contrast. Queensland colleagues were as lavish with their time as the
British Council was with mine.

And so the tour got into its stride. Armidale in New South Wales, a
small university in a remote place surrounded by forested gorges
where the wattle was in full bloom, must have found me even more of
a problem, but never showed it. In the usual austere student hostel I
was ensconced in my room for long hours of writing, the last evening
meal being high tea at 6.30. In Canberra I was kindly looked after by
the distinguished historian of the Commonwealth, Keith Hancock,
and his wife, for whom (when he was in London University) I had
once built a little house in the Chilterns. I fell in love with that city,
unfashionable in architectural circles, on account of its champagne air
and beige and blue mountain setting, in which I went for long walks, a
thing never done by urban Australians, who seem to be obsessed by
snakes and tarantulas. By now I was in love not just with Canberra but
with the whole vast country, with its American sense of opportunity
and its British sense of privacy. But I knew we were too entangled in
English education to be able to pack up and move. This was another
wayside station I must let pass.

Melbourne was much less easy. It was the eve of the Melbourne
Cup, and everybody else in the Melbourne Club, that caricature of a
frowsty old Pall Mall establishment, was slapping one another on the
back and buying rounds. The boozy racket, unexpected in the
surroundings, went on far into the night. The two universities really
did not want to know about my visit, needed no advice from England.
So after a lonely day I set about making my own social life around
bright architects like Robin Boyd and Roy Grounds, who had mutual
friends in London, and was shown the liberated and structurally
ingenious houses they were building in the richer suburbs. There
followed a weekend at Geelong Grammar School to address the boys:
staying with a sadly unassimilated English headmaster and his nice
family on a bleak campus that reminded me of my prep school. Then
off to Tasmania, trim and green, rather like Perthshire, after the
mainland's umber landscape of ragged eucalyptus, of indeterminate
"paddocks" haunted by the skeletons of burnt trees. A non-event in

Melbourne, I was a hit in Hobart, and when I had done my stuff a free-lance airman flew me over the mysterious forests of the south-west, where the sticks of fallen trees overlie one another like a game of spilikins, and set us down on a blindingly white strand beside a peaty lake where he claimed to be the first human ever to have set foot. The sun an arc-lamp, the silence lunar. The forest as we flew on was like a badger pelt, hoary with the white hairs of dead trees. The great rain-forests of the world, lush and broccoli-like from above, you know to team with human and animal life, each creature treading its ancient, secret track. But this is a forest of death, detritus of cataclysm, unforgiving witness of the slaughter of its aboriginal inhabitants.

Out of cool and cloudy Tasmania I flew into the first summer heat-wave in Adelaide: 103 in the shade, except that there was no shade from the blank stare of a white sky. With Rev. Jenkins (for whom I had built a house at Ewelme) I spent the worst afternoon in a wine cellar deep below ground. Vice-chancellors from earlier visits were in town on some conference, so I tried for a meeting to discuss my findings. I felt I owed this to the British Council's lavish endowment. But it was an excess of zeal, duly snubbed. So, feeling pleasantly unburdened, I took off for Perth, that remote, prosperous little city, glittering in the crystal light. I was headed home, but I had arranged with the Council to save up my first-class air fares by travelling Tourist (a dubious device) and so to bring C out to join me in Bangkok. She flew out in the beautiful, doomed Comet, only to be told that no plane was expected from Australia for some days. Half alarmed, half exhilarated, she settled into our stifling room in the old wooden Oriental, lying naked under the punkah. It was, I fear, an anticlimax on coming down to dinner to see me in the distance checking in. Bangkok was still a tinsel city, not yet wholly corrupted, the muddy *klongs* east of the river not yet wholly filled in as boulevards, the air just breathable. Thence we flew on to Angkor, since I feared it might never again be accessible. As we pottered along above the rain forests, the French/Annamese pilot of our Dakota decided to show off, and headed relentlessly for the ground on full power. This, I knew, was the end. As we passed the treetops on either side, I thought I had better not frighten C, so took her hand. In fact there was an airstrip invisible below, which he missed by a few feet and zoomed up again. The temples, some as formal as Versailles, some as numinous as works of nature, swam in air singing with insects. Then we turned for home, heading straight into the monsoon in Ceylon: an electric storm blacked out Colombo airport as we came in to land. We sloshed about the steaming island in an antique VW Beetle, which finally gave up on a mountain track above Nuwara Eliya. We were eventually rescued by a Christian missionary, riding down on her pile of tracts. A week later we touched down outside Moscow in a silent, orderly, snowbound terminal walled in by frozen forests on every side. Home for Christmas.

It was on this journey that (in Coleridge's words) "my mind became habituated to the Vast". As a child I used to run out into the park on summer days and lie flat on my back staring at the Atlantic cloudscape as it passed endlessly overhead. What I saw was not clouds moving, but the whole globe revolving. Spreadeagled, I clung on, as on the deck of a rolling ship. Now I had not merely girdled the planet, but become its resident, its familiar, a participator in its marvellous variety. What I had felt for England, for Europe, I could now feel deep in my bones for the world itself, and for its innocent and vulnerable passengers.

Ten years went by before I had time for another such expedition. This time I proposed my own package to the British Council. I had been much involved with city planning, and in 1970 it was still generally considered (incredible though this must now seem) that we were the world leaders in the techniques involved. My plan was for a tour of the exploding cities of Latin America, in which I would describe how we were handling the exploding south-east region of England, which was expected to have to accommodate five million more people by the end of the century. Both the Council and I had learnt a lot in the last ten years. Instead of the inadequately prepared and casually planned Australian circuit, so prodigal of time and money, I now had exactly the month of November for five countries, and a lot of trouble was taken studying the market and refining the time-table. There was a security factor (kidnapping was highly fashionable and I had a special briefing at the Foreign Office), and there was an exhaustion factor, both physical and mental, to be taken into account. For my part I worked hard, with the help of Wilfred Burns in Whitehall and Hubert Bennett at the GLC, to make sure I could put up an impeccable show that would do our country credit.

Then we set out, C dropping off (and getting lost) in Kennedy airport for a visit to Doll, with whom, over the years, she had had a long, loving, dotty correspondence. I flew on to Mexico, arriving late at night to find my luggage lost. From the air the vast city blazes to all the horizons, a spectacle which even the night sky in all its glory cannot emulate; but on the ground, it was just another hideous motorway. I awoke (did not awake, was too chilled to sleep) in a luxury quarter, richly vegetated, the sun struggling through a pearly mist. Outside, a pleasant tang of ozone must be, I thought, something to do with the altitude. It was in fact the smell of the pollution layer, which accounted for the pearly mist. Mexico seemed a sombre old city, with its maroon and crimson pumice-stone walls framed in dark-grey stone — Manchester in a foggy April. I dined in an even richer suburb, further out, with a German collector of pre-Columbian figurines. Unbearable numbers of them lined the walls. Outside, in the pearly moonlight, security guards shifted their feet and their automatics in the shadows.

Three days later, all lectures and interviews done with, came the revelation. David Thornton of the Council drove me out to Puebla. We climbed fast out of the smoggy city on its lake bed and emerged into paradise. Ixtaccihuatl, the majestic snow-covered volcano, rose up against the pale-blue sky, its feet in the mists. The quality of the air at 10,000 feet was indescribable. Flowers as bright as jewels encrusted the rolling prairies and huge butterflies like white handkerchiefs pottered about against a rich backcloth of pine forests. We spent the afternoon exploring the village churches of that region, brightly tiled like Byzantine reliquaries, their forecourts aflame with marigolds for the approaching Festival of the Dead. Then I caught the 1.30 a.m. Avianca flight to Bogota. My diary takes up the story:

BOGOTA

Where are the Andes?

Like landing at Prestwick on a wet morning.

Utterly not as preconceived.

The city's grey towers pile up faintly against an indigo mountain range, richly dark-green with wild woods at closer range. Clouds wander in its tops, or blanket it out in downpours of rain, which wash landslides of mud and rocks into the main streets.

My host's modernist residence, miles out of town in a romantic eucalyptus grove, is in a swamp alongside a millionaires' country club. You squelch ankle-deep into the funny non-grass lawn. As darkness falls the power fails and we murmur by candle-light — he worried, restless, she diabetic and even worrieder, the tiddler Jason a squeaky poppet.

Mad traffic, Africa-style pop-art buses, miles of treeless by-pass.

But the big surprise, the houses: red brick, English, beautifully detailed, terraced, Welwyn but better. The whole feel and look of lots of Bogota is English, in a Celtic landscape. Nice small urban spaces, newly paved and well-landscaped, with marvellous tropical trees silhouetted against the rainy escarpment. All the town statues are mini, absurdly small; again, English — the opposite to Mexico.

Men always in dark suits: serious; capable. Never a hippie, but thugs and petty thieves everywhere. As in Mexico, privately armed men stalk the silent suburbs at night.

On a day off, you can hairpin down 7,000 feet into another world — steaming jungles, ferociously flooding brown rivers — and lunch overlooking a blue, blood-warm pool ornamented by somnolent, beautiful weekenders from Bogota. But the dramatic drive was somewhat spoilt for me by an ex-German from the university, who near killed me with talk. This is the occupational hazard of this carefree and privileged style of travel. I had leisure to grow very fond of grey Bogota on its green plateau in its saucer of indigo mountains, and was sad to have to move on. The airport was enlivened by the scarlet ponchos of the Avianca girls. I used the long flights between the capitals for thought, for silence, for recuperation. As each sun descended into the Pacific on our right, we became a part of spectacular Turneresque skies. On the left unfolded the immense cloudy Cordillera, a great white pyramid occasionally unveiled.

LIMA

Such a history; such a disappointment. Miles of dull avenues, equestrian statues on roundabouts, tawdry stucco architecture, sky-signs, wedding-cake villas in dull expensive suburbs, heavy office blocks and hotels.

The police whistles sound like tropical bird calls.

Flat roofs everywhere, and when you get above the slum ones and look down, you see them covered with dusty junk-like attics, for it never rains. From the air — Baghdad.

The barriadas on the hill-sides, with their straw walls or mud walls painted duck-egg blue or green here and there, are a lot more attractive than the vulgar city.

The Embassy, where I am shyly met by Hugh Morgan, is over-scaled and utterly English in a dull way. I share a bathroom with a Sloane St couple. But then, going down, I meet the ambassadress, the fantastic Alexandra.

In the streets, the typists are squat, the shops low-grade, the traffic intolerable. From the BC office tower, the city looks no better: dirty-white, dusty, formless against the moon-like back-cloth of dust hills. It so needs and so seldom seems to see the sun.

The unbelievable, unrecordable, prostrating shambles of my town-hall lecture, faithfully endured by a small band of solemn devoted planners and my intelligent interpreter, Ernesto Paredes.

Next day I lunch with Peter Land whose PREVI self-build project is the most hopeful thing yet for the real housing problem in half the world. After a rushed supermarket omelette, he impatiently glancing at his watch, we rush off to his very with-it international office. I express genuine admiration all round.

Nothing in Peru, says Freddie Cooper (red-bearded and lively Peruvian architect who interprets for me), has any continuity: each new government feels it has to re-invent institutions, because the governing class has abandoned ship. Too many laws; too few customs.

CUZCO

Cautious steps as one descends into the rarefied air, and from then a permanent low ache at the front of the head.

Brick-red city 12,000 ft up in a bowl of brick-red hills, one of them carved by squads of soldiers in giant letters ARRIBA PERU. Suburban houses all of red adobe, plastered and painted pastel shades where they face the streets.

Central streets granite-paved, narrow, straight, overhung by deep eaves, with modest stucco palaces atop the impeccable, immutable, plastic Inca masonry, each stone slightly convex.

Arcaded central square in which Indian families solemnly pose to wild photographers with Vic equipment vainly trying to get them to smile. Later, a woman's soft smile as she looks intently at the developed picture. One sees any sign of joy with relief, as with the children. One sees for the first time barefoot men walk past in rags.

The 3 kinds of woman's hat: bowler, panama, lampshade. For the high white panama always a black band in mourning for the Inca.

Bent men under sacks, beasts of burden born to this for centuries.

A fluffy white tame llama eating carrots at a shop door.

At dawn, with my companion, a modest and charming architect from Lima, I boarded the little local train for Machu Picchu. It starts on the high plateau, contouring still higher along the abandoned Inca terracing, then plunges into deep and darkly forested gorges, huge leaves brushing the windows. In the misty depths you disembark and transfer to a minibus which labours up the vertiginous mountainside, to emerge in full view of the mysterious settlement perched on its high saddle and guarded by an assemblage of fantastically steep, jungle-clad peaks, appearing and disappearing in the morning mists — the landscape of a dream. Exploring the beautifully contrived, curvaceous terraces we had the space and silence to ourselves. High in the heart of it is a temple-like enclosure defined like a tiny Stonehenge by smoothly fashioned, beautifully jointed monoliths, each framing a wildly romantic prospect. The stone shapes all around have the strokeable humanity combined with the numinous mystery of a Moore masterpiece. They fitted like a glove the slim body of a ten-year-old girl who attached herself to us and to them. We ate our lunch overlooking what my diary underlines as the *most beautiful thing I have ever seen*, then coasted down in our bus. A small boy in a brown jersey, nipping down short cuts, appeared uncannily ahead of us at each hairpin bend.

SANTIAGO

I land too soon after a blissful flight along the snow-streaked Andes floodlit by the setting sun.

Peter Davies is again the urbane, charming BC type, with tall, blonde, shy wife.

The city, on its heaven-sent flat side sheltered by the great wall of the Andes, is shoddy, Victorian, down-at-heel. The only things I like are the political murals (Allende has just won) on every spare run of wall: they introduce just the colour and pop note that's needed.

Lovely peaceful embassy in a bosky suburb. Toby Hildyard very friendly, keen, intelligent; Millicent sharper, more like me. We dine à trois very pleasantly but I drink too much whisky and sleep badly.

Apart from the murals, the only rather attractive feature of Santiago is the slim girls, such a change after the stocky Peruvian workers. There's not one building worth recalling, though the group of planners led by Astica and the CIDU at the Catholic University in its charming *estancia* produced lively discussion, much sharing of views, and a sense of happiness in the Mediterranean air.

The London lecture, delightfully interpreted by pretty Ximena Rojas, goes fine, but I stood for too long at HE's subsequent long dinner-party and next day have a back-ache that ruins everything. May it go. We (led by Astica) take a long painful drive in a truck through the fruitful central valley to look at a dud housing estate. Weather impeccable. Then p.m. visit a seedy sch. of architecture — almost down to Indian standards. A group sits silent, interjecting nothing, while I converse with the Head. I long to go.

At dinner with the Davies's in their park-like suburb, ex-foreign minister Gabriel Valdès dominates the talk, a subtle, powerful man. His musical wife, Silvia, v French, delightful, but I sit next silent Mrs D and a cheery old Bohemian sculptress Marta Colvin, whose snug studio we briefly visit next brilliant morning.

Then on, my back breaking, to Valparaiso, where we call on the local government planner in a street like Lombard St. A good chap, optimist. The city is glued in tiers to steep slopes, much nicer than Santiago.

Lunch with antique endearing Br. Consul, Mr Kendrick, in his decayed Vic mansion on a hilltop. Suburbia creeping up on him, but he still potters around the exotic plants from his scandalously large estate in the southern lakes.

On to the Echeñiques' totally glamorous ocean-side cottage. I plunge with intense relief into their (freezing) pool. She looks like Sophia Loren, walks like a cat, speaks next to no English, daughter married to Valdès' son who is at present at E. Anglia Univ. Her smaller, less flamboyant, elder sister I find charming, as is Echeñique.

Cold night — roaring eucalyptus fire.

On the rocky islet opposite the Valdès' house live 2 families of penguins, on opposite sides of the island, different species, never communicating. Seals. Flocks of pelicans glide by. A condor?

Humming-bird hovers on the terrace. Back bones of whales. The hostile, icy, savage Pacific.

Callers come and go but I lie flat on the hot sand, nursing the back.

We drive home through a landscape of pure gold, with shadowed mountains and far high snows.

POLITICS
Mexico City
    We must wait for the new President
Bogota
    Reform through fear
Lima
    Grin and bear it: no alternative
Santiago (surprisingly)
    Business as usual. Among the Liberals, a sensible insouciance; among the Right, flight.

In the usual impeccable dawn I am driven along the foot of the Cordillera and over a pass to Los Andes in its (at last) green and fruitful valley. Off I go in hellishly bumpy 20-mph mountain train on 7½-hr non-stop crossing of the Andes. We climb up the grey Aconcagua river, glimpse the nameless great snow-peaks, sniff the cold air at 12,000, and descend hour on hour through a painted desert like the bottom of the Grand Canyon. Magnificent till exhaustion dulls the senses. At Mendoza, the first oasis, change into the spiffing air-conditioned EL LIBERTADOR (Italian import). After a rackety overdone dinner I stretch out luxuriously and lie drugged and soundproofed till 9.30.

Peter Hewitt meets me, I have a quick tour of Buenos Aires: see Echeñique's not wholly good Chilean Embassy, and dotty expressionist Bank of London and S.A. and miles of commonplace streets. The great 6 July avenue ruined by commercialism. The jacarandas everywhere momentarily adorn the huge and pointless city. Then I fly on.

RIO

Slept badly in the fantastic fake Adam embassy: vision of doctors, antibiotics etc. Gave up thought of Brasilia wh meant a call at 6. But seeing the sun in the shutter decided to go. Floated in embassy Rolls to close-by airport in bright morning, seeing familiar Rio landmarks.

Brasilia almost surrealist sense of space — enlarging or diminishing the human-being? Horizons all round, sky-scrapers on vast red platforms against the sky. Empty mile-wide roads to the skyline. But the central symbolic objects are terrific, life in the *superquadros* acceptable, the dark girl who took me round proud and happy like an Israeli. The dull bread-and-butter English side (shops etc.) fails, the transport network seems to have been miscalculated, but the *grandeur de l'espace*! Even the university seems to be over a mile long. Met some local archts at a buffet in a flat, then fled.

My terrific one day in Rio, fortified by throat lozenges. A.m. an intelligent young archt motored me around, showed me that plain 17c ch with its gold interior, then dropped me at Pareto's planning office. On a bench waiting (we were late as usual) sat a quiet little man with a moustache like a retired French colonel. Not introduced, he finally stood up and v modestly said "my name is Lucio Costa". Over a noisy lunch in a fish restaurant on the waterside the 3 of us had an interesting talk, of course on Brasilia etc, Costa persistently refusing to be interrupted by the rather impatient Pareto. Then LC took me off to climb up easy and delightful stages the ramped slope he has designed to the little white Gloria church. When you reach its big flat paved platform, it's much bigger and grander than you expect and has a subtly curved Borromini-type plan. Grey granite and smooth white plaster. Then down to the famous Min of Ed, for which LC led the team, and wh is still the best building in Rio. Dear fellow.

Then various confusions, including a mad visit to the office of Mauricio Roberto in a St John's Wood-type suburb, where pretty girls ripped through millions of slides of his work at breakneck pace while others tried to interview me for the Press. Zany, but fun.

BC inefficiently provided no tpt or company to my lecture at Reidy's handsome Min. of Mod. Art, so the dashing ambassadress (Greek) thumbed me a taxi and I arrived late (as usual). A mute, small, young audience had no questions. Mindlin took the chair with some charm, looking at his watch at intervals as he was due at the embassy dinner-party.

We rush off, sucking lozenges, and there is a dinner for 40 in the great white-elephant embassy. Millions of tycoons with expensive wives beautifully *soignées*: diamonds galore. I sit next a rather sweet New York Arab, the Moroccan ambassadress, who says what rot this all is. From my end of the table it looked like some Lawrence of a dinner given at Apsley House in 1830. After, we descended to the hideous and hellishly noisy "night club" they have contrived in the cellar. *Not* what the doc ordered. I retire as early as decent.

Henrique Mindlin, an unimpressive but sensitive man of 60, English in his modesty and pragmatism, collects me and I thank the Hunts and say goodbye to the vast Embassy without regret. He drives me in his small car up through the rain forests, full of red flowers and orange butterflies, to join the tourists on the Corcovado. The city is as unglamorous as possible in the dead light. Then we head downtown, buzz up one skyscraper (his) to meet his international and delightful assistants, then buzz up another, his best building, concrete and straightforward, and look down on Rio from the heliport on the roof. I photograph the party back in the busy lunch-hour street, and thence to the airport. The beautiful VC 10. So we fly off across the bay; and the pearl-white city looped around its peaks and beaches, and all my friends, and this continent no longer a mystery, are gone in a matter of seconds.

I never expect, and seldom wish, to return anywhere, but within two years I was back in Santiago. This was the doing of Gabriel Valdès, who was now in New York as Allende's representative at the UN. He seems to have persuaded the President, now eighteen months into office, that I was the person to advise him on the planning problems of the capital city. This (as will later be seen) I was really in no position to do, so I set about drumming up colleagues, only to be told that I must go alone, and let Allende have a preliminary appraisal at the end of a week. The UNDP would pay — tourist class, no fee. I was curious to see the new regime in action, so off I went into the Andean winter. On my arrival the young Minister of Planning treated me to a Marxist lecture of ominous insensitivity, but thereafter things swung along, the general atmosphere of euphoria, hard work and dedication reminiscent of the early days of the New Deal. My Chilean secretary worked her head off, and so did I: it is amazing what you can do in a week, given the right people. But Allende had to cancel my appointment: he was already in deep trouble with the transport operators, and the shadows were gathering. It was agreed that I would return after Christmas to get down to the problems of the city centre in detail. But that too had to be cancelled, and within eight months he was dead.

It must have got about on the South American grapevine that there was a London planner ready to supply you with a strategy for your capital city at the end of a week's work for next to no money, because in 1975 the UNDP invited me to do the same job for Governor Arria of Caracas. Diego Arria was thirty-six and had only been a few months in office. He was a small man of immense charm and energy, dramatized by a limp and a silver-headed cane. Politically a populist and temperamentally an autocrat, he was said to be next in line for the Presidency. The problems of city planning, I well knew (to judge from a note I made at the time), are more political than technical.

CARACAS: hypotheses

1. Administrative and boundary changes will be needed and physical plans will need to be updated.

2. However, neither plans nor reports will be worth having unless they can be implemented before they are themselves overtaken by events.

3. Any effective proposals to deal with the planning crisis in Caracas must involve:
   (a) Restrictions on the freedom of landowners to do what they want with their land.
   (b) Restrictions on the freedom of citizens to do what they want with their cars.
   They will therefore be unpopular.

4. Unpopular measures are best introduced in a package that contains popular ones also. The opening of the metro will be an opportunity to do this. The package must therefore be prepared now so that it is ready then.

5. The Governor has almost unlimited power to do popular things. Power to do unpopular things must rest on public understanding and consent. For this the ground must be prepared now.

6. Foreign methods and experience are of very limited value in matters of this kind.

7. I therefore need to understand the historic and contemporary roots of democratic power in Caracas, what natural communities

and groupings exist, and how they are or could be expressed in institutions and by individuals.

I also knew that other planners had had a go, notably Colin Buchanan, who wrote to warn me that Arria was an impossible man to deal with. As soon as I arrived in Caracas I went to his home for a cup of tea, and found him distracted, giving, as is often the way of politicians, only half his mind to the subject. Spoilt children got too much of his attention, his beautiful wife, who strolled in in an impeccable riding habit, too much of mine. There followed days of exploration and of interviews with suspicious officials, a lot older and stuffier than the *jeunes féroces* of Santiago. On my side I had the generous support of the British ambassador, Jock Taylor, an energetic diplomat of the new hard-headed school. Caracas is an immense arena of urban drama, with the millionaires playing their skyscraper games on its floor overlooked by two million Oliver Twists perched precariously on the steep slopes of the surrounding mountains. Half a million cars infest the city like maggots and strangle the peak-hour freeways.

At the end of my week I met C in Barbados and wrote my report⋆ under a mango in the garden of Heron Bay, Ronnie Tree's Palladian villa, designed by Geoffrey Jellicoe and built of pale coral. I read it to Marietta and to Richard Llewelyn-Davies, whose partners were already familiar with Caracas and would, I hoped, carry on where I left off. I then sent it off to Arria with a complimentary letter. It was never acknowledged, and sank, like so many other such documents, without trace. I had to assume that it did not back up the policies he had already decided to pursue.

My fondest memory of that assignment was of the young architect, Gonzalo Castellanos, who accompanied me the whole time as a kind of amanuensis. On a Sunday picnic expedition into the magnificent landscapes south of the city, he and his English wife and I found we saw the world through the same eyes. I liked to think that this, and other such experiences, were a mutual recognition of E. M. Forster's "aristocracy of the sensitive, the considerate and plucky", transcending frontiers. But perhaps the special charm of these passing relationships suited my taste for the tangential reference rather than the plunge, and my perennial desire to be off and away.

⋆See Appendix: a planning curiosity, demonstrating what you can do in a week, and what you cannot do even in one of the few Latin American democracies.

Chapter eight

THE CENTRE OF THINGS

IN THE SPRING of 1960 came a letter from Francis Pollen. He had
worked at Watlington in the early fifties, living with his delightful
black-haired wife, Thérèse Sheridan from County Mayo, in one of the
attic flats, where their first child, Clare, was born. Later he had set up
in London with his cousin, Philip Jebb. But their practice had not
prospered, and he wondered if I would like him to come back, plus his
clientele. This put me on the spot. Francis came from a distinguished
Catholic family and his parents were friends of ours —Arthur a
sculptor, Daphne a painter who had spent childhood summers on
Lambay island in one of Lutyens' most romantic houses. Francis
himself had grown up in the shadow of Lutyens, yet was as
determined as I had been to break that mould, which I was confident
he was talented enough to do: he was a born architect. I was also
immensely fond of him. But just as immensely was I enjoying my
release from partnership: my tiny team in the cowshed was the right
size for happiness. But (again) I also knew that I had more to do in
the world than this modest back-up could support. I had neither the
temperament nor the talent for a country GP, still less the genius of
the loner. Both my limitations and my ambitions pointed me
towards the problems of cities, the dilemmas of planning, the politics
of architecture. The decision was inevitable and I never regretted it.
Francis gave his skills and his dedication to his clients and to mine,
while I was sucked irresistibly into the whirlpool of London.

My own exit from the world of the New Towns coincided, as it
happened, with a public need to divert attention from them to the state
of the inner cities. The New Towns had had it easy: swimming with
the tide of everybody's desire to move out, they could hardly fail. To
achieve for the old "twilight areas", with their miles of collapsing
houses and backyard industries, an equivalent standard of life, which
was the final objective of the New Towns strategy, was going to be
much harder. If we were to avoid the brutal solution of dropping a
prefabricated tower block on to every pocket-handkerchief of

ground, we must spread the load more evenly across the conurbations. This meant exploiting some of the wasted acres in the vast expanses of inter-war suburbia for more compact housing — an invasion of *Daily Express* territory by *Daily Mirror* people which we should have known was a political non-starter in the Britain of the early sixties, or indeed in any Britain one can easily imagine. But this did not deter me and my friends from having a go in lectures and newspaper articles and pressure groups and elegantly designed but little-visited exhibitions. "Build in the messes we have already made," was the cry.

Nothing came of all this. Indeed, nothing much came of such modest planning consultancies as came my way. Maidenhead preferred to cut its inner ring road through working-class housing than to widen an ugly commercial street lined by the business premises of leading citizens. Abingdon decreed that I must look for my fee to the commercial developers and the architect they had already engaged, so that I could only secure such cosmetic treatment as they were prepared to wear. Shaftesbury, conned into engaging me by the fund-raising enterprise of Rolf Gardiner, a high-minded and far-sighted local landowner, did nothing. Plans for Buckinghamshire commuter villages commissioned by their excellent Planning Officer, Fred Pooley, came to nothing when development pressures were correctly siphoned off to Milton Keynes. At the other extreme of size, plans for a new community of 20,000 people on the northern fringes of Southampton, which we took down to the detail of individual house designs, were abandoned when local elections brought in a Labour majority ideologically committed to such jobs being done "in house". But my two most spectacular non-events were in London and in Corsica, and these come later in the story.

For some years, until he was approaching eighty and the deafness which he had feigned as a defence against bores became real, my father and I shared out the committee work, myself on occasion taking over from him. He did the National Trust, the Society for the Protection of Ancient Buildings, the London Museum and a lot of work for the theatre,* I the RIBA and the Royal Fine Art Commission and the Georgian Group and the Council for the Preservation of Rural

*He extracted its first million pounds for the National Theatre from Hugh Dalton, and would perhaps have had one of the three theatres named after him if he had not had to sack Laurence Olivier for absence without leave.

England. Altogether he seems to have been mixed up with some seventeen such organizations in the fifties and I with a similar number in the sixties. He was better at it than I was, both funnier and more formidable, exercising those privileges of age. I tended to impatience, never quite free of an awareness that all such work was secondary to the overriding purpose of any artist.

Voluntary work is generally harmless and often therapeutic, despite the violent rows it occasionally engenders. One must have faith that its benefits outweigh the brake it often is on the wheels of action. My father was without cynicism and had no such reservations. Because he knew he was good at it, he liked chairing things — even a society dedicated to rescuing Victorian buildings he intensely disliked — provided he could get away when he wanted to. Increasingly he cut out winter meetings so that he could sit on the sunny terrace of the small house they had bought at Châteauneuf, overlooking the coast from near Grasse. Here they were looked after by tiny indomitable Edith and by a rather shady manservant and his wife who managed the household accounts. He played the part of an old man with gusto, enjoying an occasional illness or operation as a chance of flirting with nurses. Other people's illnesses he did not want to know about. He liked scoring off the Revenue, considered that in justice he should only pay surtax on his net income, and was determined to die penniless, leaving my mother to sort out the consequent debts and the chaos left by his eccentric accountant, Mr Percy Popkin. The thing he would find hard to take about being dead, he said, was not getting *The Times* every morning.

And thus in 1963 he did die, at Châteauneuf, after an agonizing 24 hours in which my mother was alone in the house with him, unfeelingly neglected by the local doctor. By the time we could arrive she was her usual sensible self, seemingly accepting a widowhood that both of them had always anticipated — she was six years younger than he, and her father had lived to ninety-two. But the deep shock of his death, and the greyness of life unsupported by his delight in it, as well as her incapacity to cope with the "dull things" he had always managed, rapidly undermined her iron constitution. She fell a victim to rheumatoid arthritis, struggling up stairs she had so recently rushed up two at a time. Illness and pain were new experiences for her, and she bitterly resented them. The following summer she was persuaded by a friend, Frances Phipps, to go to Bad Gastein in Austria for a "cure", but she refused to follow the prescribed regime. Frances sent us long, desperate reports. "When the blight of Boredom comes down on her it is like an iron curtain that shuts out People completely and makes her live in a loveless world — an air I cannot breathe. . . . she has got so used to Edith's devotion and unselfishness that she takes for granted (like a little girl) that E can stand anything and forgets how old and frail she is. . . . It is almost unbearable to hear the sort of things she says — so bitter and so indifferent to the claims and feelings of others: she does not *know* it upsets people . . . I cannot reach her heart, she has put it into a sort of Frigidaire and shut the door." It was intolerable to her that she should have to join what Frances (who had herself been a member of it) described as the Fraternity of Pain. There were moments when she felt that she had failed with her children, and could not repair it, and these sharpened the bitterness.

Yet this dark portrait cannot be the whole truth. She was a faithful and affectionate correspondent and to the end continued to exchange long letters with old and new women friends. But even the newest, Lyn Irvine, then a sensitive young writer married to a Cambridge don, is now dead. It must be a common experience that we are too self-centred, too busy, to try to understand our parents' natures until it is too late and all the evidence has gone.

For some months she struggled on at Turville, then was transported to a private hospital in London run by aloof nuns. On the M40 I overtook her, so as to be there when she arrived. In her glass ambulance she lay expressionless, like a figure on a bier, but without the serenity of death. I felt heartless passing her thus at speed. Perhaps we all felt — in this respect were — heartless. Love was what she desperately needed, but all we could give her, doing our stints at the bedside, was duty. Only Edith, taken, and taking it, for granted, remained easy and familiar to the last.

All four of our parents died within those four years, Olive after eight years of gallantly borne frustration following a thrombosis which affected her speech but not her intelligence. Only C, with the intuition she had inherited from her, had been able to get through to her, despite all that she herself, not yet out of the wood of anxiety, had to contend with. Being both of us the eldest, we had to sort out an unbelievable mass of possessions. There was first Olive's London studio to be disposed of, with hundreds of canvases and sheaves of drawings; then my parents' rooms in Albany, C having conceived a dislike for the superior porters and claustrophobic Rope Walk: she infinitely preferred her studio in a secret garden in Battersea. Then my mother's neat house at Turville, with its ladylike countenance and vast labour-intensive garden — not our scene. Next came Eben's cottage in Sussex, chock full of stuff from larger houses. Finally, after struggling for two or three years to find tenants for it, we had to pack up and sell the French house, a decision I regretted for years. Like all those who go through that experience, which often strikes at the high tide of other business and children's problems, I resolved that henceforth I myself would travel light.

The children were by now all in their teens and twenties. It is hard to write of them, each one as hard to pin down as the subject of this book and, like it, enfolded by history — the start in life of the eldest (Eton, Magdalen, Grenadier Guards, the City) and of the youngest (Bryanston, Goa, Katmandu, rural commune) summing it up. In these terms, they belonged to three generations. The two eldest were pre-war, pre-dating as school-leavers the arrival of the Youth Culture from America, though the police were just beginning to harass hippies while Michael was an architectural student. The two war babies were of the generation of Marcusian alienation. Guy, seeing art in political terms, dropped out of his job as art critic of *The Times*; Sebastian fell among Vietnam draft-dodgers and became a sociology lecturer at York, later giving up this tenured post to research the shanty towns of Bogota. Chivalrous by nature and nurture, they have always found waifs irresistible. Both eventually, after other vicissitudes, married beautiful Chilean refugees. Olivia and Stephen belonged to the age of the flower children: Stephen was ten when the first Beatles disc came out and sang their songs in the back of the car all over the west of Ireland in 1966. Romantics too, they are nevertheless well endowed with the good sense of a generation that has come round to riding the roller-coaster of the world as it is. Perhaps all six have more in common than these pairings might suggest — generosity and constancy, for example: they are not the ones to run out. Of their dozen or so "relationships" only one, way back in 1962, was solemnized in church. All except Olivia are now married to Americans, north or south. All are learners and loners, tending to escape from organizations, in reaction, inevitably, from the pursuit of "success".

They are united in another sense, as the first generation in centuries of English history to grow up unencumbered, or uninspired, by any concept of national purpose or of the power to pursue it. They belonged to a class which had hitherto considered itself in charge not just of this country but of the world. If it failed in crisis management, there could be another world war. When the economy collapsed, as in the thirties, it was its job to think out a better system and its role to bring it into being. By the sixties there it was, this better system, with full employment, social security, a health service and housing and planning achievements on which one could lecture without embarrassment all over the world. But by the time it in its turn ran down, power had moved elsewhere and feelings had taken the place of thought. Revolution by demo, the drug culture, inner enlightenment and the loneliness of nihilism, all of them long since discredited in Russia, were now on offer from France or America. Our children could not for long buy these, and with most of their generation found themselves driven out of the public sphere into the private — into the

nomadic civilization which is altering human nature so profoundly, and throws upon personal relations a stress greater than they have ever borne before. Under cosmopolitanism, if it comes [continued E. M. Forster, writing in 1908] we shall receive no help from the earth. Trees and meadows and mountains will only be a spectacle, and the binding force that they once exercised on character must be entrusted to Love alone. May Love be equal to the task.

Love proved unequal, except within tiny circles of friends and family, and society went on its frightening, perhaps fatal, way.

It was as I took my seat in the Presidential chair for my first RIBA Council meeting that a message was put before me that my mother was dying, and this was to be characteristic of the stresses of those years. We both took life at a run, C weaving her way like a wing three-quarter through the scrums of Selfridges, I glancing at agendas at every red traffic light. Often, running to a meeting from a remote meter, I would trip up and land in the gutter, attracting anxious passers-by, whom I irritably waved away before limping on with a grazed knee. Once, gravely discussing the state of architecture with a young journalist on some country walk, I tripped over a root and executed a perfect somersault in mid-sentence (a skill I had developed playing Fly in the Field Game). He looked at me as though at a mad old gentleman in a Lear limerick. In this world, a crowded engagement book was a success symbol, the most successful being he who was unavailable for lunch for the longest stretch ahead. My secretary, Miss Syms, a cosy white-haired countrywoman and mother-figure in the cowshed, had to learn to compete on the telephone with glossier ladies in swinging London. As Johnson remarked of John Wesley: "His conversation is good, but he is never at leisure. He is always obliged to go at a certain hour."

We now look back on the sixties as a decade of unprecedented and probably unrepeatable prosperity, creativity and high living. In fact its middle years were marked by economic mismanagement and the usual "cuts", always first felt in architecture. "Even before the present cut-backs," I moaned in my Inaugural Address in 1965, "there never seemed to be enough money for anything . . . I find it hard to accept that we are the first civilization which has known quite clearly what it needed to do, wanted passionately to do it, possessed all the techniques to do it, but been physically incapable of the necessary effort." In the speechifying I had to do all over the country in those years the themes were always that we had to be more professionally flexible and more technically ingenious if we were to do more with less in the hard-up public sector, and if we were to assert ourselves over the booming private sector, which was making a killing in our city centres. My *bêtes noires* were the package-deal tower block and the speculative office developer, and I everywhere preached low-rise housing and more money for conservation and conversion. I was also much concerned with what the spec. builders were doing to the villages, and we made the best of a thin time in the office by producing in 1965 a picture-book, *Landscape in Distress*, illustrating what was happening in Oxfordshire. The key, we could all see, lay in local government, where a vicious circle operated: it was dim and dull because bright people would not go into it; bright people would not go into it because it was dim and dull. Walking round the playing fields of Churchill College at Dick Crossman's spanking pace I urged him to set out on the notoriously thorny path of local government reform and with a groan he agreed he must. The Maude Commission in due course proposed exactly what we wanted, only to have its recommendations disastrously turned upside down by Peter Walker.

The job at the RIBA was of course to some extent ornamental, and among the chores least enjoyed by successive Presidents (architects being the shy people they generally are) were the full-dress dinners organized by regional societies in provincial cities. Swaddled against back-ache like a Chinese baby I would shake hands with hundreds of architects and their guests, then process in to dinner to the ironical slow handclap which the British affect on these occasions. C, at the peak of her beauty, dazzled the Lord Mayor or the Lord Lieutenant while I jollied along the shy Lady Mayoress. After-dinner speaking, which all sorts of Englishmen do so well, I do badly, handicapped by having had so witty a father — the kind of man (like Hugh Casson) who made people smile simply by rising to his feet, so that when he was due to speak in the House of Lords peers came crowding in from the bars and tea-rooms. He enjoyed teasing the big parties on both sides. Thus, helped into his fur-lined overcoat by some life peer, "I wear this coat inside-out," he said, "as a concession to you Labour fellers." Remoter places were easier to please. I was the first RIBA President to visit the Channel Islands and Hong Kong, where to our astonishment the airport terminal building was festooned with a giant banner of welcome. I must also have been the first to chair an annual conference in Dublin (hosted by the *Royal* Institute of Architects of Ireland) in a condition only to be described as pixilated after a ravishing, timeless fortnight in the far west, swimming here and there in the icy Atlantic. Total aphasia was the embarrassing symptom. On these jaunts we were accompanied by the charming, anxious Secretary, Gordon Ricketts, who only a year later fell tragically to his death from Beachy Head.

To escape pursuit I had to get away from Watlington, and we always went *en famille* to North Wales. As I was a sort of sleeping director of Portmeirion, Clough used to let us use White Horses, the most isolated of his cottages, occasionally flooded out by high tides. But we longed for a nest of our own and in 1964 he led us to a heather-covered rock, entirely surrounded by trees, which he claimed could be opened up to overlook the estuary. There was just room on it for a one-room dwelling, and here we built a little place which externally was acceptable to him and internally is like a great wooden tent. Aligned due south on Harlech Castle, its vast view, when the curtain of trees was drawn aside, was a revelation, and remains flawless to this day, untouched by one new building. From here I climbed every peak in Snowdonia by every conceivable route, swam in every inlet, and with Liz Beasley wrote the *Shell Guide to North Wales*, wildly rushing about the wildly unreliable scenery to catch some photograph. It is impossible to imagine a more enjoyable holiday task. It was a joy when John Piper, our old friend and neighbour in the Chilterns, who edited the guides, let us do it, particularly since it was virgin architectural territory which even Pevsner had never penetrated; and it gave me a chance to record my feeling for that landscape — greater than for any other, except of course for those landscapes that are for ever made numinous by love.

Clough and Amabel made use of the surplus farmhouses and cottages he owned up the Croesor valley and on the Portmeirion peninsula to attract a circle of writers and artists, generally left-inclined in varying degrees, which was as refreshing as the Atlantic air. Its doyen and star at the frequent parties in and around Portmeirion was Bertrand Russell; and even Arthur Koestler, in those sadly few years when he was married to Mamaine Paget, had bought a farmhouse nearby, though he disliked the Welsh and felt a fish out of water — or a soaked cat *in* the water that endlessly descended upon their windswept ridge high up in the Ffestiniog valley. As he and I stood talking on some rock there his hair and mine (such as it was) were seen to stand up vertically on our heads as an electric storm approached. Other intermittent *estivants*, perched on the steep slopes that led up to the peak of Cnicht, were the superbly handsome physicist Patrick Blackett, with whom Amabel could converse on terms of intellectual equality, the elfin painter Fred Uhlman with his English wife and even, rarely, the bewitching Christabel Aberconway, for whom Clough had converted an old mine building overlooking a vast panorama. Down on the peninsula were, in addition to the Russells, four permanent residents and dear friends: Micky Burn, the wayward and amused writer who had been our "best man" in 1935. Captured and sent to Colditz after the St Nazaire raid, he had married soon after the war, and brought to a remote cottage beside a waterfall, the beautiful Mary Booker. Her face was a piece of perfect carving and she had a sense of fun that was not statuesque at all. For some years Micky ran a mussels business on Portmadoc quay too generously, so that it ended in bankruptcy. The other two were Rupert and Elizabeth Crawshay-Williams. He was a logical positivist of the school of Ayer, she equally clever, but content to read, bake cakes and converse in her witty and pleasantly malicious Irish way. They had settled in their low-ceilinged cottage in the war, when Rupert, in revolt against a reactionary family background, had taught in an evacuated prep school in Deudraeth Castle. To everybody's surprise, they had remained content with this withdrawn existence tucked away behind the Welsh mountains, Rupert making only occasional forays in his fast car to lecture in English universities. He would stride the vast sands at low tide, with their over-indulged dog, tape-recording a book or a passing thought. He was addicted to electronic gadgetry, most of all to recorded music. Both had an intense interest in people, particularly the young, loved gossip, loved theorizing, hated cant. They were incapable of self-deception, and when Elizabeth, after years of increasing deafness which nobody noticed because of her brilliant lip-reading, became incurably ill, they decided the time had come to end their lives, young though they both still seemed. One Sunday morning in 1977 they were found dead in bed together, an unforgettable shock to their neighbours and friends. Portmeirion for me can never be the same again.

We lived, of course, only on the fringe of that Portmeirion world, or indeed, I often felt, of any other. Like my father (and, I think, his) I tended to flee from secure male-dominated societies like those of University, Army, Profession etc., preferring the company of women, or of similarly unclubbable men. Always on the wing in London, I could not, for example, adapt to the tempo of the Beefsteak, which unlike other clubs he enjoyed and got me into. We were to be found nearer the edges of several intersecting circles rather than in any of their centres, unlike my sister Pinkie, who was herself, amused and amusing, at the still centre of the unstable literary world of London, such as it now was. That was one of our fringes. Then there was architecture, where my background tended to distance me, particularly when, to the embarrassment of the radical element I admired, I suddenly had to change my name. Indeed, in some circles you could never live down that handicap. Then there were the neighbours at Watlington, landed or exurbanite: to the former I was no doubt myself a left-wing London intellectual. There were C's shooting friends, notably Peter Fleming, who admired her springer spaniels second only to herself, and her Jungian friends, who regarded me as incurably Apollonian. And later, as will be seen, there was the "art world", of which I could only ever be an honorary member, as might be an American on sabbatical.

It was in these same fringes that we found our closest friends — our eternally disappointing, disappointed, friends, for the facilities that enabled friendship to flower and last no longer existed. Did such a person as Desmond MacCarthy still exist, or had his style of talk, his incapacity to meet a deadline, his vast store of reading, been frozen out by interruptions to stack dishes, television, noise from low ceilings, office hours? We were, I suppose, a dull generation, distracted by crises, excessively busy, sandwiched in between two (by design or accident) more leisurely ones.

In 1965 there was change afoot at Watlington. That autumn one of the huge eighteenth-century beeches blew down on the edge of a small clearing in a remote and unkempt corner of the park where scouts and guides occasionally camped. For some time now, in a desultory sort of way, I had kept an eye open for a site to build, against the day when we would hand the old house over to the next generation. Once or twice I had noted some spot and planted a few trees to protect it from the tireless winds that infest our escarpment. Now for a variety of reasons it seemed that the time and place had arrived. C was exhausted by the house, I by the garden, which never seemed manageable however much I let go. The sweat of it all, the threat of new taxes which would make the transfer impossible, settled the issue. Characteristically of the period, I had in mind a glass house on *pilotis*, where we would live a part of nature in our bird-loud glade. C would have none of it. She would only live among these towering oaks if I lifted her high into the air. So we built a five-storey tower, a Dark Tower with a moat, so she could sleep at squirrel level — only halfway up the trees, but with prospects between them of the hawthorn jungle foaming out to the horizon. Bracken and deer come right up to the moat, and after fifteen years those who come on it at dusk must think they see a survival from centuries ago — a watch-tower better adapted, I suppose, to the world's neo-medieval state of mind than the Forest-of-Arden idyll I had imagined.

This had to be the end, too, of the Watlington architectural commune. Most people by now lived outside, and the sort of clients we were now getting — bankers, insurance companies, big London estates, city corporations — could not be expected to appreciate the rustic charm of the team in the cowshed. In the competitive world of the sixties we just looked (though we were not) amateurish and undercapitalized. We were certainly hard to pin a label on . . . Harry Teggin for example. One soaking autumn day two newly qualified architects, tough, stocky Merseysiders, friends and rivals, squelched in for interview, smelling like wet dogs, having hiked the three miles up the scarp from Watlington Station. We liked both, and both were first-rate. But Harry would brook no rival and in a short time had established himself as a key figure in the office. In the early sixties I had been brought in by an architect friend, Jeff Mathews, to replan with him the Sloane Street/Cadogan area for Lord Cadogan. For the then black canyon of Pont Street I had the hereditary snobbish contempt of one brought up in the white stucco world, and proposed we knock it for six by removing the central block behind the trees on the south side, putting there a tall red tower on the axis of Hans Place, and on the spot where Sir Hans Sloane's architect, Henry Holland, had built his own centrepiece, the Pavilion. The long dull stretch of Sloane Street itself we would split into three, with two business ends and a residential centrepiece, the latter achieved by bridging the street with buildings at the top and bottom ends of Cadogan Place. Under these bridge buildings you would enter a unified and noble space on the scale of the Palais Royal. Rightly, as is now thought, nothing came of these or any other of our ideas. Instead, Sloane Street was to be rebuilt piecemeal and we were asked to set the tone. We produced a dark, bricky building they call Fordie House for the central residential square (on the roof of which we lived for ten years), and a cantilevered glass office block, to be rented by Miki Sekers, which made it possible to widen the bottleneck of Harriet Street. Harry designed the latter and ran the job impeccably, but Cadogan's tastes were Georgian and he disliked them both. The example they were supposed to set was anyway later flagrantly ignored by Jacobsen's posthumous Danish Embassy, which imported into our bricky residential square the high-tech atmosphere we had proposed to keep out of it.

It was these subtleties of atmosphere and problems of relationship that fascinated me about our trade. We were handling the difficult combination of a revolutionary architecture rooted in a new technology on the one hand, and on the other an historically unprecedented concern for the world we had inherited. Often my advice to new clients was to do nothing, or do the minimum, and what I liked about the Tower was that it dropped into a scene that seems to pre-date the human race with the absolute minimum of disturbance, like the extraordinarily delicate elephant's footprint in the bamboo forest. (This was the way childhood insecurity had taught me to move through life.) But we puritanically rejected pastiche: however pictur-esque the village, our new cottages were unmistakably 1960. Delicacy of the kind we cultivated has its obverse. With the hindsight of the more rhetorical seventies some of our stuff looked pusillanimous and dull. Exeter College's new building in the Broad at Oxford, with its tower at one end to match the others in the Turl and its attic carried across from Scott's at the other, was perhaps a case in point. A self-contained *palazzo*, making no concessions to neighbours, would have been equally in order. But Oxford gave me stage-fright. King Street in Manchester, on the other hand, a collection of grandiose commercial palaces ranging in date from Cockerell to Lutyens, is a traditional free-for-all. Here Casson and Conder were to build alongside us a monolithic granite bank, so we took the female part, with a many-faceted dark building, concave in response to their convexity, rather in the way that their Royal College of Art courtyard responds to the vast rotundity of the Albert Hall. Both buildings won awards and for ours Harry deserved and got much of the credit.

He was (is) a romantic, who with his wife had run a youth hostel in the Highlands as a prelude to architecture, with a Napoleonic streak that was bound to land him in trouble as well as triumph. In those days, like Carlyle, he saw a few people as heroes, most as fools, and I was never sure which category I came into. When we finally took the plunge and moved the practice to London, where my old friend Geoffrey Jellicoe offered us house-room in Lutyens' old office at 17 Queen Anne's Gate, he made no bones about the category Geoffrey's staff belonged in; and he would march into the private offices of Chairmen and Chief Executives and give them hell. I put up with this for years, because I had a high regard for his professional competence and lively imagination: we had (have) a lot in common. Francis could meanwhile immerse himself in his own jobs, completing with his octagonal Library the series of buildings at Downside we had started in the Boyd and Bosanquet years, building his monumental church at Worth, a good Barclays Bank in Newbury and several private houses. But partners' meetings tended to be stormy and at times the set-up seemed headed for another break-up — a hard thing to contemplate or manage with each of us responsible for jobs that can last for ten years.

The plan for the new city centre at Portsmouth was a case in point. I was appointed in 1963 and our new Guildhall Square was finally opened by Lord Mountbatten in 1976. Portsmouth had naturally been heavily bombed in the war. The city centre, which lies close to the

Dockyard, had been devastated and the grand late-Victorian Guildhall reduced to a shell. Twenty years later, when it had been rebuilt, donkeys still grazed on wasteland a few yards from its great Corinthian portico. The job was to divert the heavy traffic that passed its steep flight of steps and replan and rebuild the whole of the ravaged 38 acres around it, embodying such Victorian architecture as had survived. From the start it seemed to me a solecism to align some new civic axis on the Guildhall portico — better to contrive its gradual revelation by an oblique pedestrian approach on the model of the Ludgate Hill approach to St Paul's. We could then build a new setting for the Guildhall in the form of a square on two levels, setting up a monumental bronze figure of Queen Victoria that had stood nearby in the centre of a wide flight of steps between the two. This would face the portico and incidentally make a grandstand for naval parades and other processions. All this came to pass largely through the strenuous advocacy in the early days of Freddie Emery-Wallis, then Leader of the Council. Much argument went on in Queen Anne's Gate about the design of the Civic Offices that embrace the Square. Social and aesthetic considerations pulled opposite ways. The pleasant thing, I thought, would be a long bricky range with everything openable, sun-soaked, natural ventilation: no Kafkaesque mysteries about what went on inside. The finer thing would be a reflective bronze glass building (not then a cliché) divided into tall bays scaled to relate to the bays of the white Guildhall façade. Since it was the sixties, the sealed glass building won, and since it was England the air-conditioning failed to work. It looks good, but it looks aloof. Even the cafés and boutiques we wanted to open on to the Square were sacrificed to office space. The 1974 oil crisis arrived with the contract only half let, but Harry characteristically saved the day by persuading the builders to lend the money for the other half. The slump since then also killed off most of the rest of my brick-paved city centre, but the half-loaf is something.

In 1967 what looked like an even more protracted operation arrived in the office. The French Government had decided to build a New Town on the east coast of Corsica. This was not to be just another set of Languedoc-type white concrete holiday ziggurats, but a working town for a population of 25,000, intended to attract industries and immigrants, particularly the troublesome *pieds noirs* from North Africa, a few of whom were already settled along this remote, beautiful coast, almost uninhabited until endemic malaria was recently brought under control. The Planning Ministry in Paris, which was to finance the infrastructure of the new town, at that time looked to Britain for planning and development expertise, and the project had been entrusted to a syndicate which had already engaged my brother-in-law, Martyn Beckett, now an excellent domestic architect. He in turn asked me to do the town-planning. I was briefed in a noisy and chaotic office on the Boulevard Haussmann — the sort of accommodation French Government Departments then still occupied. Soon I was off to Corsica, called on the not surprisingly suspicious *préfet* in Ajaccio, then drove to the site. It was a landscape of pure magic, such as I did not know still existed in Europe. Behind an apparently endless and completely deserted white sand beach were tangled forests of pine and broad-leaved evergreen set on little hills sloping down to great silent, peaty lagoons. In the background a line of snowpeaks glittered in the May sunlight. I could see at once that what lay ahead was not just a new job but a new life.

Over the next year I explored the wild and romantic island from end to end and we and the Beckett family stayed in bad hotels in magnificent situations. The surveying and planning went forward: I chose the site, looking across a lagoon to the mountains, where we would spend a third of each year for the rest of our lives. In the May of 1968 Martyn and I went down for a routine visit, during which we heard rumours of some student riots in Paris. Then the whole Air France system was grounded. We each got a lift in private planes, mine only as far as Nice. Pacing the airport there, wondering what to do next, I caught sight of the painter Louis le Brocquy, who generously took me home to their white-shuttered house at Carros. There, in continuous rain and that strange suspension of life that attends such dramas, the three of us waited for the *événements* to resolve themselves. But a few weeks after I got home news arrived that the chastened de Gaulle Government, with so much to do on the mainland, had decided to scrap the project. Perhaps that lonely shore remains inviolate.

Distraction from disappointment was provided by the publication that summer of my report on York, which I had finished writing on Christmas Eve. Two years earlier, impressed by the public outcry at the damage done to the heart of Worcester by redevelopment, Crossman had decided to commission some studies of major historic city centres as exemplars of how such places might survive the stresses of the twentieth century. After some argument with local authorities, not all of whom wished to be Whitehall guinea-pigs, I was offered the choice of Chester, Bath or York (Chichester was to be done by its own Planning Officer). York, I was told, would be the most worthwhile but difficult as the City Council was hostile. So I chose it, on the understanding that this would not be just another exercise on paper, which I had had enough of, but a live demonstration, with Government money (two million was spoken of), of conservation and renewal in action. My arrival in York fulfilled all expectations. I was smuggled into the Guildhall by a back door for fear I might meet the Press, then told by Mr Burke (railwayman and leader of the Labour Council), in his solid Yorkshire drawl, "we don't like consultants here". The Conservative boss was if anything more unfriendly. Mr Bellhouse, the City Engineer and Planning Officer, was correct, but inevitably resented my appointment as a criticism of his department's performance. However, we set up an office in Micklegate and got busy, with Harry in charge, David Lloyd on historic buildings and Nat Lichfield on the economics. Citizens high and low, academics, professionals, students in large numbers, were roped in. As the months went by and our proposals were gradually unveiled at public meetings, allies and enthusiasts materialized. The most stalwart was John Shannon, Chairman of the York Civic Trust, a passionate lover of the walled city and a splendid speaker. I sometimes wondered whether his enthusiastic advocacy, like Mr Gosling's at Hatfield, might turn some people off, but I soon realized that he knew his people and they knew and trusted him. The support of Archbishop Coggan, as President of the Trust, was also much more than *ex officio*. Another essential ally was the local paper, the *Yorkshire Evening Press*, and eventually as personalities changed on the Council and among its senior officials I found friends there too. We never got the Government money, so implementation had to wait upon the rates and upon the market, but over the years John Shannon has taken care that each civic improvement, each Trust conservation or restoration project, should be seen as an instalment of "Esher". I still hope that the last two big things, the removal of Deangate, a misconceived Victorian short-cut which swamps the Minster with traffic, and the redemption of the horrific surroundings of Clifford's Tower, may happen in my time.

On the flyleaf of the York report I quoted in huge letters some words of the Dutch architect Aldo van Eyck:

THIS MUCH IS CERTAIN: THE TOWN HAS NO ROOM FOR THE CITIZEN — NO MEANING AT ALL — UNLESS HE IS GATHERED INTO ITS MEANING. AS FOR ARCHITECTURE, IT NEED DO NO MORE THAN ASSIST MAN'S HOMECOMING.

What was at stake, I thought, was more than "conservation". It was to reverse the flight from the cities that had been in full swing for the last hundred years, and nurse them back to life. It would be done by returning the heart of the town to the human being on foot, by creating or reviving an enveloping central space, and above all by bringing people back to live in the centre of things. In the Middle Ages a population of ten thousand had lived within the walls of York in the usual European pattern of close-packed houses with large green spaces at their backs. Now it was down to three and a half. We planned to bring it back to six. But it was fifteen years before I opened the first group of houses to be built on our model, and at this rate it would be 50 before the job were done. In the case of Portsmouth seven years passed before any new buildings were started and after another seven only half the job was done; the rest, as is customary, had been abandoned or compromised.

In the winter of 1968–9 I wrote a book pretentiously called *Parameters and Images* in which I tried to foresee the role of the architect, the "geosophy" he would need, in the world culture that seemed to be emerging:

It is more than one building thick, or one profession thick. The individual cell, the building, the group, the community, the city, the region, the land and water surface of the globe — in this nexus, which we had better not call a hierarchy if that implies degrees of importance, there is no break-point anywhere. Nor is there any break-point between the natural and the artificial environment. We live, we know, in a space-time continuum in which we are all both subjects and objects: we change it, and it changes us. In this continuum, construction equals destruction, and the only meaningful word is *change*. If it was once useful and meaningful to write of architecture as an isolable element in the ordering of change, it is so no longer. We can only write of the art of change.

Doll at Taos

Watlington, 1960

C and the children

In the garden

The reclaimed market place at Abingdon

Olivia photographed by Anthony Gascoigne

The Tower

We shall succeed in this art not by learning its theory but by understanding its material — or more simply not by Learning but by Understanding; and first, by understanding the world. In this world, in which we prospered and multiplied by exploitation, we shall only survive by striking a proper male/female balance between development and conservation.

That I should have had time for this book was a sign that I was under-employed. That I was under-employed was partly because the role I wanted hardly existed. True, I had a fleeting chance in South America to demonstrate, up to a point, that this was not mere planner's rhetoric. But in the Britain of 1970 it was a fantasy. Nevertheless its presence in my mind made it hard to concentrate (for example) on our efforts in the Royal Fine Art Commission: I was torn between my affection for it as a group of friends and my impatience with its forlorn task of making silk purses out of sow's ears. Only rarely did the architects' magic, that can transform experience, come before us. More commonly the scene he created, after such effort and anxiety, was not as interesting, as photogenic, as human, as the scene he had nothing to do with. It was the quarrymen's town of Bethesda, not Portmeirion, that one wanted to draw and photograph. Could it be that what an artist finds moving or significant in the physical world an architect can rarely confer, and must often destroy? To this day, whenever I pass an illiterate block of flats in Exhibition Road, or the Royal Lancaster Hotel, or the violated silhouette of the Palace of Westminster seen from the South Bank — all cases where we either failed to visualize or were ignored — I try without much success to recall what we did achieve, to justify our often embarrassing bossing about of other architects. When after eighteen years I was suddenly told between meetings that my tour of duty had ended I minded the manner of it but saw it made sense. It was absurd to imagine that the architect could hope to influence the physical world on the scale that interested me.

He never had, and looking at the vast sprawls of American-style cities, now spreading all over the world, over which (except for a few down-town landmarks) he had virtually no control, it did not look as if he ever would. Certainly the days of the independent planning consultant were numbered. In Britain, as it turned out, he was only a stop-gap until such time as the planning authorities had set up (as a

result of our own pressure from the RIBA) properly staffed departments qualified to do the job themselves. Those few city-centre
planning consultancies that were still put out to the private sector were
anxiously contested by the half-dozen firms which had set up the
expensive multi-disciplinary resources you needed if you were to be
ready at a moment's notice to take them on. In this high-powered and
highly competitive market, much of which was now perforce having
to look overseas for customers, our little outfit in Queen Anne's Gate
was small fry. Such situations tend to be divisive, and I was tired of my
role of front man, job-getter and conciliator in this crew of a small
boat searching for a non-existent North-West Passage. It could not be
an accident that not one of our excursions into town- or city-centre
planning reached its objective. I began to think it must be a Faustian
fantasy to suppose that the infinite intricacy of the human anthill could
be disturbed without instinctive resistance. It simply closed round us
and carried on. I seemed to be coming out on the far side of
architecture.

Some years before, I had been asked by Robin Darwin, its Principal,
to do a stint on the governing body of the Royal College of Art. It was
a largely ornamental role: we sat round and listened to projects and
problems he and Colin Anderson, his charming and sensitive
Chairman, had already decided how to handle. But I had caught the
general euphoria the place then exuded, and still occasionally dined
there. One such summer evening in 1970 Reta Casson, whom I
gratefully sat next to, told me that Robin had decided to go in a year's
time and that they were in the midst of the search for a successor. Why
didn't I have a go? Without a shadow of doubt I knew that this was
what I had to do. One hot and heavy July day I walked through
Kensington Gardens to the interview, dodging from tree to tree for
shade, then back to C's first one-man show at the New Art Centre,
where she sold pretty well everything. A new life seemed to be
dawning for both of us.

Chapter nine

BACK TO THE FRONT

THE ROYAL COLLEGE of Art is a monument to the determination of men of taste to do something constructive about the vulgarity of the consumer products of the Industrial Revolution. The objects of the report of 1835 from which it originated — to boost exports and improve the quality of life (in that order) — have the familiarity of the Irish problem. Not for want of trying, we seemed to have a blind-spot for both. Through the rest of the nineteenth century the Central School of Practical Art (as it became in 1852) was to be the centre of a network, unique in the world, of nearly 200 art schools. Thousands of portfolios were examined in the studios attached to the grandiose Victoria and Albert Museum, then vanished, as did their authors, without trace. The quality of life in 1896, when the School became the RCA and handed over its control of national art and design education to the local authorities, was, if anything, worse. A much larger population lived and worked in worse cities, in buildings in which no architect had had a hand and among artefacts on which trained designers had had no influence. By then the Arts and Crafts fraternity had found an answer, and when one of its leading lights, W. R. Lethaby, became Professor of Design in 1901 it seemed that the work-bench rather than the life-class might at last become the designer's *milieu*. But he failed to get his workshops before the 1914 catastrophe. Between the wars his influence faded, and in the thirties, with Sir William Rothenstein as Principal, the College was unashamedly a prestigious art school, making as little impact as ever on the industrial scene or on the counters of Harrods.

Robin Darwin had been at school with me — a formidable, hirsute fellow who produced powerful cartoons for stained glass in the Drawing School and (cast against type) played the flute at school concerts. Born into the Cambridge establishment that had dominated English intellectual life between the wars, he accepted the appointment to the College in 1948 on condition that the whole of the teaching staff placed their resignations in his hands. The people he

then brought in to head his new specialist Schools — Goodden and
Guyatt, R. D Russell and Casson, Madge Garland, Skeaping,
Moynihan — were friends or friends of friends, who set that collective
tone of elegance, wit and nice manners which the 1951 Festival and
then the Coronation briefly elevated into a national style. The latest
machinery was installed in the Western Galleries by newly engaged
white-coated craftsmen — Nature's gentlemen — and splendid
commissions began to roll in from leading architects and born-again
businessmen. By 1965, when Bryan Robertson and John Russell, in a
huge coffee-table volume called *Private View* illuminated by many of
the cleverest photographs Snowdon had ever taken, celebrated our
great new Capital City of the Arts, the College had become both very
smart and very professional. Beautiful upper-class ladies served on the
governing body and it was a feather in anyone's cap to be asked to
lunch in the dark-green Senior Common Room, described by
Robertson and Russell as "a mixture of High Table and grand country
house". Robin missed nothing — his shrewd eye at the service of an
inborn sense of how things should be done. They were not always
done without pain and drama, for he had a heart that could
disconcertingly be either hard or soft as his feelings dictated. He had an
easy mastery of the English language which he sought manfully to
instil into the increasingly illiterate output of the provincial art
schools. With these Churchillian qualities he combined a romantic
reverence for science and technology, the converse of the scientist's
deference to Art, and was specially proud of the "hard" side of the
College's activities. Its prestige, and the sense of excitement that
pervaded it in the sixties, were a remarkable personal achievement.

But increasingly as the decade advanced the base of the pyramid, the
students themselves, began to wobble. As early as 1959, in a section of
his Annual Report headed "The Beat Generation", Darwin had
remarked that "the student of today is less easy to teach because the
chips on his shoulder, which in some instances are virtually professional epaulettes, make him less ready to learn". No less dispiriting
were those lank-haired girls in their colourless, waist-less clothing,
and the alienation from RCA values given expression in the unintelligible, anti-art graphics of the College's once immaculate *Ark*
magazine. But so long as "the skills were there" he could be
philosophical. "Considered more or less in the abstract there is
something engaging and admirable in this attitude and one cannot

help thinking of another age in which a revolt against increasing luxury and profligacy scorched Europe under the magic hand of St Francis of Assisi. . . . I have no doubt at all that it is we of an older generation who by some lack of discipline perhaps or by some failure to define the boundaries of belief, have left the young with so little sense of direction" — paternalist sentiments that were soon to date.

In 1970, depressed by poor health, shocked by the quagmire of nihilism in which some young artists seemed set on sinking, above all warned by a sure political instinct that student politics were about to pass beyond his patience and his skills, he decided to go. When he heard that I was available he moved to support me with an enthusiasm which (as on previous occasions) I feared might be counter-productive, despite his long experience in getting his way. But I suppose my equal enthusiasm settled the issue. Not that I had any illusions about what I was in for. The previous November *RCA Newsheet*, a student ephemeral, had published a characteristic news item about my exalted opposite number in Bloomsbury.

On October 21st fifty London University students demonstrated outside Senate House, the University's administrative buildings, to protest against the assistance that London University gives to University College, Salisbury; to demand the resignation of all governors of London University colleges who have investments in companies which trade with South Africa and Rhodesia; and to demand the resignation of Douglas Logan, L.U. principal, for condoning the situation.

On arrival at Senate House all the doors were locked and behind them were thirty university officials. The students were told that they would not be allowed in to see Logan. After some harangue about producing union cards, ten students were allowed into the building, and apparently were set upon by the officials and porters inside. Both sides allege that the other started it. It seems impossible to disentangle exactly what happened, but several students were badly bruised and shaken, and one student was taken to hospital with throat injuries.

It also seems that photographs were faked — Dr Pownall, clerk to the senate, fell to the ground before students were anywhere near him, and up popped a handily placed photographer. Obviously Logan had expected a much larger demonstration; the police were in readiness just around the corner. They apparently stood back while the students were beaten up, and then arrested five whom they took to be the ringleaders. These five were taken to Brixton. They have been in prison for two weeks.

Hock and Gillespie, both Americans, face probable deportation if convicted. Demonstrations are planned outside and inside the courts when the arrested students are tried.

This issue is not simply an internal affair of London University, but part of an attempt by students to fight against racialism at all levels of society.

Student violence, like everything else, had made its landfall from America.

I had a year to get organized. In the autumn I had to research and fly off on my Latin American lecture tour. On my return I read the whole literature of "design" — easily done because (unlike architecture's) there was not much of it. I toured the College with Robin. What, for example, was my opinion of Environmental Media, Light Transmission and Projection as an art form, let alone an academic discipline? I hadn't the foggiest idea, except that this avant-garde ghetto, with one part-time tutor, ought not to be isolated in a Kensington Gore attic but down the road with the rest of the artists. But neither Carel Weight in "painting" nor Bernard Meadows in "sculpture" had the space, nor the slightest desire, to take it on board — a typical RCA impasse. Hugh Casson sent me one of his comic sketches showing himself sucking his teeth over *RCA Redefined*, a student union publication demanding all sorts of reforms designed to combat Apathy and Absenteeism, which was causing some nervousness among professors — so much so that I decided to address a general meeting of students in the summer before I had officially even arrived. I was myself nervous of my Etonian, House of Lords image and thought it wise to establish liberal credentials — probably a mistake. To my embarrassment, Robin crept into the gallery to listen, and in a P.S. to a subsequent letter shrewdly advised: "*Surtout, pas trop de zèle!*" Yet he was at pains to impress on me the weight of the Rector's work-load — "a seven-day-a-week job". I did not see how I could combine this with architectural responsibilities (for which experience had given me a lot of respect), so I left my practice to Francis and Harry, who later predictably parted company. The day on which they signed an indemnity absolving me of all future responsibility for what went wrong I felt like a ten-year-old on the first day of the summer holidays.

I found the College schizophrenic about what should happen next. "This place needs a shake-up," said Dick Guyatt. But I knew that the Darwin tradition, soon to be the Darwin legend, would be sacrosanct for years to come. Meanwhile, *RCA Redefined* was unfinished (unbegun) business. I thought the best way to move on it was to set up a two-day talk-in organized on conventional conference lines, with the 300 or so who chose to turn up split into half a dozen staff-student syndicates, each with chairman, rapporteur etc. Most of the student demands — more mobility, more personal tutors, participation in all decision-making (including entrance exams), more flexible courses, no honorific prizes (only cash ones), looked easy to me, and it was noticeable that none of the staff wished or dared to diverge from the prevailing sympathetic liberalism. Eating arrangements were the sticking-point, probing deep into archetypal attitudes. The present set-up was a sitting target. It consisted of a three-storey building, with the students (other ranks) eating like troglodytes in self-imposed squalor at the bottom, NCO's (technicians, secretaries etc.) in the middle, and the elegant Darwinian Senior Common Room, so beloved of outsiders, on top. This was easily shelved by taking the view that a flexible horizontal rather than a rigid vertical layout was the answer. I described it, with deliberate vagueness, as having "a soft end, a hard end and plenty of space in between". This, of course, could only be achieved when we got a new building. To go on with, I asked Reta Casson to devise a less austere, less echoing environment for the students' canteen, but it was refused. Like Palestinian refugees, they did not want their alienation undermined.

So the eating problem was genuinely divisive, and would not go away. To the staff, scattered in their tiny "schools", the Senior Common Room was a place to meet colleagues, a place to get away from students, and, most usefully, a place to entertain College (and other) clients. A handful of egalitarians went slumming occasionally among the troglodytes, or invited one or two up to lunch. And in the evenings the SCR bar was in its early days open to all; but students did not care for its style or its prices and the staff had gone home, so it had to shut down for lack of custom. For, like all institutions in the expensive heart of London, we were a nine-to-five, five-day-week establishment. The staff neither wished nor could afford to live close by and most commuted vast distances to log fires in the Home Counties. The students on the other hand, sleeping in cramped and lonely digs, did most of their work in the evenings. To visit the Schools in working hours I had the choice of a stultified C.O.'s inspection or an impromptu call when I would find the benches deserted, except perhaps for some serious painters whose deeply introverted territories (they liked to wall themselves off even from one another) I had not the courage to invade. We were a long way from being the "academic community" the more socially conscious students dreamed of, and to which they saw the communal lunch-hour as the locked gate.

All the same, we made progress in other directions. "Participation" had not yet fallen into disrepute, so I pushed it as far as it could go. The Oxbridge-style JCR now became the Student Union, with representatives, heavily "mandated", on every committee and involvement in every decision, including staff appointments, with the sole exception of the personal fortunes of individual students. The key, I thought, to good management was my relationship with the S.U. President, in which I hoped we would both know that we each had a role we were obliged to play. Of my first, a swarthy fellow who looked like a 1920 caricature anarchist and always cut me dead in public, I wrote:

> Your role is to attack, mine to defend
> A world that in its rough and ready way
> Has mothered both of us; yours to expose
> Its antique bestialities, as though
> Just excavated, mine to turn away;
> Your shield is truth, my cloak hypocrisy.
> Your role is hate of me, mine love of you,
> And — what's so funny and so sad about it —
> We both are such implausible performers.

My second, Brian Webb, one of the moving spirits of *RCA Redefined*, was a radical idealist who wrote essays with titles like "The Bitter Taste of Living" and whose show of work for his degree consisted solely of Agitprop, yet whose last words to me when he came to say goodbye were: "You know, I love this place." I felt then that my policy was working. Better still, Olivia told me her friends thought so too. The policy was, of course, to isolate the irreconcilable minority by a genuine effort to enter into the minds of the majority. One of their preoccupations was the College's involvement with those "oppressive capitalist forces" for whose sustenance we had originally come into existence and whose good opinion Robin Darwin had been at such pains to cultivate. All the universities now had to check their investment portfolios for South African or other racist connections; we had to check our commissions as well. Even a design for a new policeman's helmet caused much heart-searching in the School of Industrial Design, and the Experimental Cartography Unit was thought to be a front for the CIA. The only respectable clients were Third World agencies or handicapped people. In the 1973 Design Oration at the Royal Society of Arts, which gave me a chance to put the case of the young at some length, I spoke of "a sense of futility in making minor design improvements in machine products like type-writers or telephones when the world is running out of raw materials, a sense of guilt in helping vast international companies to promote, write off and replace luxury products when half the world population doesn't have enough to eat".

Even though I described it as a half-truth, this was heretical talk, since it put our national role and Government support at risk (as the College was later to find). It was unashamedly a bid for the support of student opinion, without which, sooner or later, we would be in trouble. My summer vacation work for Allende was part of the same bid. I probably overdid it. It is hard to draw the line between a necessary effort of the imagination and over-identification due to nervousness or sentimentality. Inevitably the more conservative saw only the latter. Robin Darwin used occasionally to lunch in the Senior Common Room, sitting in his accustomed seat at the "painters' table". (I, of course, had no such prerogative — did not believe in having it.) He wrote disarmingly to say he hoped I would not mind: these were his oldest friends. But it must have been hard for him to close his ears. In due course the counter-reformation got itself organized, and an emissary called on me to say they regarded me as a disaster for the College — a conversation stopper if ever there was one. A meeting of teaching staff was called to set up some sort of protection association. I was sure that if I addressed it I could stop it in its tracks, and I suppose they thought so too, since they would not admit me. So in despair I walked out of the place and joined the zany, irresponsible strollers in the King's Road, who were not in the business of organizing one another.

Yet there were times, not long before and not long after, when looking around at lunch in the speckled sunlight of the SCR I would say to myself: this is the best place on earth, and these are its best people. In that same speech at the RSA, in an attempt to put this feeling into words, I spoke of

> fundamental things I believe we teach in this country, or rather communicate. It may embarrass you, or remind you of the Beatles, if I say that the first is love — that love for people in general, for the people we pass in the street, that we all feel when we are *in* love, but can lose when we are out of it. I hate the arrogance of so many architects, designers and even some artists, a vice almost wholly absent from the great artists of the past. Creative people, as they like to describe themselves, are in no way superior to anybody else, whatever the media may say. We will be better artists for cultivating that total submission to the needs of the particular problem, that refusal to cheat, which is the hallmark of professionalism. We used to be told, when we had ears for it, that perfect love casteth out fear, and it doesn't even have to be perfect to do that, and to dispose once and for all of that fear of the young which is even more damaging than the Victorian deference to the old. But the contemporary return to the medieval idea of the university as a community of thinkers, or anyway of talkers, is a great gain, because talking is learning. We work by talking towards a consensus upon what is relevant, because of course we have to pursue this quest, however silly our attitudes may look to the next generation. And by relevance we mean relevance to our inner selves, not to society, or success, or productivity — on Ruskin's principle that "the only wealth is life". I have in mind here what Ivan Illich calls a "convivial" rather than a "manipulative" institution, an institution that is oriented not towards goals but towards relationships, not towards growth but towards stability.

Finally we try to communicate as best we can the continuity of human experience and our own society's capacity for non-violent change. If Newton, congratulated on his achievements, could explain, "Ah, but I stood on giant shoulders", we ought not to be above making the same acknowledgement.

★

Wandering through the annual Degree Show as the students set up their wares, beside which they would sit for days on end like merchants in a souk anxiously waiting for Mr Right to walk up, it was impossible not to be deeply moved by their creativity, their vulnerability, their innocence. At Convocation (the degree ceremony) thereafter I would mention a few by name, until I discovered that for some puritanical reason they had boycotted it. Others turned up so as to put on an act, the most celebrated the heavily moustached Darwin masks raised at a signal by the serried ranks of students sitting behind him and out of his sight. As life became more political fears increased that these jokes would go over the top, but they never quite did. The whole performance (invented by Robin) was preserved by the fact that its grandeur was heavily diluted with irony, not least in the marvellously funny citations for Honorands delivered by Christopher Cornford as Public Orator.

The counter-reformation did not last long. In the end I think what reconciled us was that everything I attempted failed. By way of diversion from internal dissension, like any politician, I switched to foreign affairs. There were two things which, as an architect, I was expected to achieve for the College. The first was an alliance or merger with, or if that failed the creation of, a School of Architecture, which has to be regarded as the central discipline in design education. Darwin had long ago taken the Bauhaus as his model and seen (as I did) our lack of one as a serious weakness. Since there were too many already it was silly to start a new one, so in the days when we had a lien on the long frontage in Queen's Gate he had offered a section of it to the Architectural Association School, on the understanding that on arrival they would become a constituent College of our neighbour, the Imperial College of Science and Technology, and a link between that huge institution and ourselves. A competition for their new building, replacing four Victorian houses, had ensued with rather embarrassing results, compounded when the AA, after a spell of the violent altercation to which it was addicted, decided it was too democratic an institution to be able to live in the university system. Having thus rejected Government endowment, the school was now largely patronized by Americans who alone could afford its high fees. Even so it was in financial straits and its lease in Bedford Square was running out. So I approached Alvin Boyarsky, its Principal, with what I hoped would be a more attractive proposition — the use of our studios and other buildings at the back of the V & A when our new building made them surplus to requirements, plus whatever loose relationship with us would preserve their freedoms. It was necessary to be quite open about this if some plot was not to be suspected, which enabled the AA to reject us with a show of *hauteur*, as though it was we who were in difficulties. So that was the end of that. It had in any case depended on our indeed getting our Phase Two buildings in Queen's Gate, to which the Government had been committed when Phase One, the great black block, had gone up alongside the Albert Hall.

Getting Phase Two out of the ground was my second task. On the site at present were some rather stodgy Victorian mansions, some yellow stucco, some red brick — a lot less elegant than the Regency terrace that had been blithely removed to make way for Phase One. But much had changed in the architectural world since 1960. Victorian South Kensington was now a Conservation Area and our Queen's Gate frontage was "listed", so we were in for a Public Enquiry. Hugh Casson and Jim Cadbury-Brown produced a rather mannered, red-brick design carefully composed to do honour to its equally mannered red-brick neighbours, and I asked Dick Sheppard to testify to its merits and Mark Girouard to testify to the mediocrity of the buildings it was to replace. They did so to such effect that the Inspector recommended in our favour. But Tony Crosland, moved I think not only by architectural populism but also by a dislike for the College's pretensions he had acquired when Minister of Education, overruled him. So an interesting post-modern building was lost to London. We had to fall back on the much less convenient site in front of the V & A, long vacant since its early Victorian terraces had been demolished in the thirties to make way for Lutyens' abortive National Theatre. But here we were up against market competition — front runner the Aga Khan with (to our embarrassment) Casson and Conder as his architects. Our scheme, by Cadbury-Brown, had to squeeze far more on to this costly site, and it was obvious that we could only win with some local government discrimination in our favour. I went to work on the Tory GLC, claiming the national interest, but they opted predictably for the bigger money and (one can now see) the better building. This was not quite the end of the story. I discovered that the five identical, magnificently Piranesian warehouses of London Dock, just east of St Katherine's, were on the market. I was convinced that if the College could summon up the courage and the cash to pack up and go there it would not only be the "shake-up" we needed in all sorts of senses but also an exciting contribution to the revival of the Docklands. I sold the idea to our Governing Council, but the staff and students, even their left-wing union, were dead against. They were the people who would have to live there, and they liked South Kensington a lot better. Soon after, as sometimes happened to listed buildings that are in the way of development, somebody put a match to them.

In South Kensington maybe, but not *of* it! Those who commissioned us to celebrate some national occasion, such as the College had done with such educated wit and consensual elegance in 1951, were in for a shock in the sour seventies. Thus when in 1973 the College was invited to design and mount an exhibition in Bath to mark the one-thousandth anniversary of British monarchy I was still naïve enough to think this was just up our street and a chance to put into practice the "cross-disciplinary communication" the students were theoretically so keen on. Such shows, with their vulnerable deadlines, are always traumatic, exhausting and a prey to blackmail. We (most of all gallant Joy Law as co-ordinator) suffered the usual prima donna tantrums, accusations of exploitation, overcharging and in the end financial embarrassment. The show itself, an uneven mix of pop art, surrealism, whimsy, caricature, skill and muddle, was good fun on its own level — until I had to take the Queen and Prince Philip round it. I then felt constrained to send a message of apology, but got back from Balmoral an assurance that "there was no question of any offence having been given".

In the midwinter of 1974 Robin Darwin died. There followed a memorial service in the vast spaces of the Brompton Oratory. His wife, Ginette, was one of my oldest friends. Could we have imagined, as we picnicked on the grass under a tree in Kew Gardens in some pre-war June, the parts that we would be playing 40 years later under that dark and gloomy Roman dome? Things were to happen before long in his beloved College that it was just as well he did not see.

Meanwhile a certain scepticism settled on me. One of Hugh Casson's sketches showed me riding furiously for some fence, himself falling off behind. I saw his point: why force the pace? At our overdone committee meetings, all of which I was supposed to go to, I always sat facing the windows so I could watch the green and gold plane trees, the buses and the crocodiles of tiny, purple-bereted girls go by. My job, it seemed, was really just to man Darwin's huge rosewood and black leather desk with its crowned phoenix stamped in the centre, so that angry or worried people or gossips or bores or accomplices could drop by. I began to realize how large a slice of how many lives is spent just waiting for something to happen. On sunshiny days, in love with Kensington Gardens, I would run across the Gore and stride the cool avenue of huge planes that runs from the Albert Memorial to the Watts statue, or the windy expanses of the Round Pond. More dutifully, to fill empty afternoons and to improve my limited understanding of art, I accepted Pat Gibson's invitation to join the Arts Council and chair its Art Panel, poorly equipped though I knew I was to succeed John Pope-Hennessey in that role. After a session with aggrieved Community Artists in Piccadilly it was a bit of fun to cross Green Park and chair the Advisory Board for Redundant Churches in the heart of clerical Westminster.

I even took on another abortive planning exercise for a doomed head of state. We were under strong pressure from the Foreign Office to accept an invitation to assist the Government of Iran to create a so-called University of the Arts on the northern fringes of Tehran. We were told that the Empress herself was to be chairman of the planning committee, that the University of California had already agreed to be associated with the project, and that the College had been chosen to be responsible for the European input. We were reminded of Britain's economic stake in Iran and of the export opportunities such a contract would open up. Conscious of political sensitivity, I hedged for a time, but by 1976 I judged the College scene tranquil enough for me to recommend Senate and Council to accept, and in May I flew out, with a young British architect representing the design consortium, to meet the academic planners and discuss the structure of the new university. Snow-capped mountains rose out of brown smog as we descended into Tehran — an oil-boom city, with all of the traffic chaos and none of the glamour of Caracas. The British Council gave a lunch in the Hilton overlooking the drab scene from the superior tree-clad slopes to the north not far from our site. But I found the Vice-Chancellor elect and his colleagues, unlike their counterparts in Santiago, exuding nervousness rather than exhilaration, creatures of the imperial will, with none of the idiosyncrasies we expect of academics. My suggestion that to the American/European connection they should add, for obvious geographical and cultural reasons, an Indian one was frostily received: it was undiluted westernization they were after.

Within these parameters we made good progress, and I had time for a day off in Isfahan, escorted by a young American-trained member of the committee. As we explored the magical city and later sat under the stars in the vast fake-Islamic cloister of a luxury hotel, he agonized about politics. Could a westernized liberal like himself breathe the air of a police state from which his left-wing friends had one-by-one "disappeared", or should he pack up and go back to the USA? Obviously the same must apply to my mission. Should we carry on and exercise such influence as we could, or leave it to the French? You should stay, he told me. You should stay, I told him. That afternoon we had been shown over the prettily planted campus-style university by an Armenian Christian official, and then, with great pride, his own little cathedral. Horrific murals of the agonies of Christ and of Christian martyrs were a shock after the peerless serenity of the Muslim masterpieces. In Isfahan Islam seemed totally benign. Yet this man, member of a tiny religious minority, feared for his future too. There was something rotten in the radiant air.

Tehran airport, jammed solid by the Shah's formidable fighter/ bomber squadrons, was a shambles. After queueing endlessly for frisking, we sat in a bus for an hour, were loaded into an aircraft, then unloaded, sent to the back of the queue, frisked again, re-loaded, but finally, in the front end of a 747, floated in silence through a dark-blue sky with the snow-covered ranges of Kurdistan glittering below us — an earthly, mechanized equivalent of the transition from purgatory to heaven.

And so the years passed. On the 23rd of February 1977 I went down after lunch to my large room, with its claustrophobic mews outlook, to pick up my papers for the monthly meeting of the Senate, of which I was chairman. I found it occupied by a solemn group of students who announced to me that "to achieve any serious negotiating power with the College Administration, they had no alternative but to take direct action". They had therefore occupied the whole of the College's administrative offices. I knew, of course, what this was all about: the Government had announced that student fees were going up. Five out of six of our students had state bursaries and would be unaffected, and we had already announced that we would look after the remaining one-sixth, unsupported students, the majority of them from overseas. So it was a non-issue, but for the militants it would have to do. I sat down at my desk and told the assembled mob that it could never win, then left for the Senate. Here we were invaded by a delegation and a statement was read to us in a barely intelligible foreign accent. David Queensberry asked the man to take it more slowly, which caused deep offence. We were told, inter alia, that students had been mandated to boycott all future Senate and other meetings.

This set the tone for the coming weeks. For much had changed since the idealistic days of *RCA Redefined*. Bored stiff by "participation", politically minded students had read their Marcuse and written off the whole exercise as "manipulation". Thus the School Forums we had set up in response to student demand were now described by the Union leadership as "an information-retrieval service for the Rector and whatever college authority mandates them, and an opportunity in case of 'undesirable' Student Union motions of recourse to extra ratifying and delaying tactic". Illiteracy, solemnity and suspicion were now in command. Leadership had emerged mainly from the departments which dealt in the media — Film and Television and General Studies — both, as it happened, under the charge of professors who were, naïvely in one case, agonizedly in the other, in sympathy with the militant position. It was also (though the weak Student President was British) markedly foreign: the proposer of the motion that "we reject the College tactics as being derogatory and negative and not forwarding any real dialogue and resolve" was called Sonheil Sleiman, the seconder Haim Bresheeth, from two of the 26 countries whose representation in the College I had proclaimed with pride as proof of our unique international standing. In fact names were rarely used: for ideological and "security" reasons the letters I received were generally signed "yours sincerely, the Administrative Committee". And of course it was all copycat stuff, imported from the PNL and the LSE, whose unfortunate Director had recently had to address a student meeting with every back turned towards him. But all we of the establishment had was an unanswerable case. Confronted by force, we had none to match it, since I knew that the College was overwhelmingly against bringing "the fuzz" on to the scene.

I now had no office, no files, no typewriter, but with my marvellous secretary, who had worked for Bill Holford before joining Robin at the College, I moved to a tiny room in the mews, where over repeated cups of tea we achieved rather a snug blitz-type atmosphere. But a couple of days later the shock of what had happened to her familiar College proved too much for her and she had to go home for the duration. I was now on my own, until Roger Nicholson offered me desk-space in his airy room overlooking the Albert Hall. This was loyal of him, since he knew that wherever I was was liable to be occupied. My best hope, as in the past, was to appeal to the great majority of political innocents. So I sent this message to every student:

It is essential in the interest of the whole College that the present disruption should be ended as soon as possible. The purpose of this paper is to clarify the situation as simply as I can.

The Royal College of Art will be under severe financial pressure in the year 1977/1978. Our estimate of the cost of running the College at its present level in this coming year is £2.4m. This figure has already been cut to the minimum. We know unofficially from the DES that we are likely to receive between £300,000 and £400,000 less than this. The main demands of the Student Action Committee that fees should remain at their present level, and be the same for British and foreign students, would add another £348,000, making a total cut in relation to need of at least £648,000. I need hardly say that this would mean many redundancies and intolerable cuts in services and materials. The College would virtually destroy itself in order to protect 503 bursary students from charges which will in any case be borne for them by the Government.

On the other hand, the College accepts that a small minority of unsupported students, both British and foreign, will be hit by the new fees, and Council has already made it plain that it is the College's policy to protect these students from any financial sacrifice.

However, the Student Action Committee is not prepared to accept anything less than a public statement by me that the College will not implement the new fee scales, though I have made it crystal clear what the damage, in every sense of the word, would be. It has also told me it will not negotiate until this public statement has been made.

This is the issue. I have asked the Heads of all Schools and Departments to call an immediate School Forum, and to let me know the view taken by their students of the action taken by the

Student Action Committee. Until this action is ended by the majority asserting itself, none of the central services of the college can operate. The effects are already being felt, and will be cumulative with every day that passes.

In a confidential note to Professors I said it was "essential that students that are opposed to what is going on should stand up and be counted . . . they should be encouraged to make immediate contact with like-minded students and requisition a General Meeting of the Student Union". This was at once leaked to the militants who published it as "an obviously naughty attempt to manipulate and split the students in order to smash the occupation" — which indeed it was. My second move, on Day Two, was to close the whole College for a day, on the pretext of a national strike of our technicians' union, the ASTMS, and of rumour that the occupation might spread. The object was to induce outlying departments to identify with their beleaguered headquarters (which I knew from Army experience lower echelons never do). This was generally thought to be tiresome and irresponsible interference with what really mattered — their work. When the School forums duly met to discuss my message professors wholly failed, or scarcely attempted, to influence them. All came out solidly for the occupation, then happily returned to their benches and easels.

So we were in for the long haul: we had to talk them down — find the formula that would let them off the hook without giving anything of substance away. Of course purists could say (though nobody did): no talks under duress; end the sit-in first. But opinion demanded action of some sort, and the anti-talk minority wanted not immobility but a punch-up. And so, following the failed Forums, five of us talked all day with five students, even though they were "not mandated to negotiate". We got nowhere, and finally Anthony Lousada as Chairman of Council offered to continue discussions only if the occupation ended within 48 hours (announced by the Union as "a clumsy manoeuvre"). The hours expired and I then played my last card — a personal appeal to a meeting of the whole student body next day. It took place in the usually elegant Gulbenkian Hall, at that moment half dark and piled with packing cases and stacks of examination portfolios on which students perched in suitably revolutionary attitudes. Having gone over the ground yet again I ended:

Over the past ten days the College has been through one of the saddest episodes in its long history, representing for me personally the failure of everything I have tried to do here. War games, like war itself, may for a brief time be an ego-trip to some people, but they leave a nasty taste afterwards. They debase us all. There are no winners, only losers, and the worst sufferers are the innocent — in this case young men and women who have devoted themselves to this place, who work a long week and work through vacations when academic staff and students can get away. They do it because they admire this College as a unique and famous liberal institution. All the greater their sense of outrage and the bitterness they now feel and have expressed to me. It runs very deep, and it will take many months to heal.

I appeal to each and every one of you who has been in any way involved to do what he or she can to restore and reassure them. Even so, you will have to live with the loss of many of the services and benefits you take too easily for granted.

Many of us over these last days have said and done things that we ought to regret, or have failed to say and do things that we might helpfully have said and done. I am among them, so there will be no preaching from me and there will be no recriminations.

But let me add this, because it isn't all negative. Many of you after some blind row with friend or spouse will know that these things can lead to a deeper understanding, to better communications, to more honest relationships. Laurens van der Post, in one of his earlier books on Africa, tells of an Arthurian legend. Here are his words:

> Two knights, one in black armour and one in white, were riding through a dark and dangerous wood in search of a chivalrous errand when they met. Vizors down because of probable danger, they challenged one another and, without further explanation, fought. They fought until they were both wounded to death and finally lay stretched out on the grass beside each other. Then, in dying, they uncovered their heads — and saw that they were brothers.

It reads well, but it went badly. Anthony and I had guessed that the militant tactic would be to swamp this emotive stuff in a mass of tricky or jokey questions, so we had agreed our best plan was not to allow any. But when the time came and the questons were called out by militants cleverly distributed among the audience, it seemed to me worse to shirk them, so I waded in. At the end of the verbal rough-house I knew my appeal was already forgotten. I also knew, most bitterly, that it was a quality I lacked, not just a mistake I had made. I was reminded of somebody's comment on Stanley Baldwin, who "always hit the nail on the head, but it didn't go in".

The occupation now became institutionalized. As with all "polit-ical" squats, well-known left-wing personalities paid courtesy calls or gave talks, including our own Guy Brett who had lately left *The Times*, and including, of course, sympathizers on the teaching staff. The pirates hoisted their Jolly Roger across the face of the building, proclaiming their prize to passengers in the No. 9 bus in the usual grotty revolutionary graphics. The Student President, his feet on Darwin's desk, organized the systematic reading of all the Registry files in the traditional hunt for political comments on individual students, and finding none, gave the Press copies of a few letters which it was hoped would embarrass us. Secretaries' and clerks' personal possessions were ransacked. They, of course, were all at home on full pay, but the stories reached them. The result was a bitter backlash stretching from top to bottom of the administrative staff and directed personally against me. We now had to decide whether to go for an injunction to get the squatters removed. The Professorial Board, my personal "cabinet", was divided and of course insecure — no place for frank discussion of policy. Two senior members of the Council for whom I had respect and affection and who had been involved as Governors in the LSE and Essex University troubles were dead against police enforcement. In the end Anthony and I decided to take some preliminary steps to save time but to stop short of final implementation.

Two volunteers now offered to have a go — Peter de Francia, an intellectual and a loner, whose appointment as Professor of Painting had been bitterly resented by the Royal Academy establishment, but who as a veteran Marxist was well-equipped to enter into the minds of the militants, whom he could not take very seriously; and Reg Gadney, a young writer in General Studies, impulsive, extrovert and known to be a "good communicator". Since both are highly emotional (and thus no exceptions in the College) I attached to them two cooler heads from the administrative staff and they got going.

After ten hours of argument with half a dozen students they emerged exhausted with an agreed communiqué of sorts, which was promptly repudiated by the Students Union. Plainly the high command had not yet been eroded by boredom (our secret weapon). But it was becoming clear that it was now prepared to pull out with a lot less to show for it than it had originally demanded. How to deliver the *coup de grâce*? It came from a totally unexpected quarter. William Betsch was a "mature student" (in the emotional as well as the technical sense) doing a thesis in the Painting School on Moroccan fountains. Like many Americans of his generation, who had seen it all before, he was politically far more sophisticated, as well as more literate, than our own rag tag and bobtail. Perhaps with some encouragement from Peter he called on me to offer himself as go-between. There ensued an extraordinary interchange of minuscule, nit-picking verbal bargaining. One evening, when I was opening a charity art show on a wet night in High Wycombe, he drove the whole way down there to get my agreement to a single word. In the end his package prospered. It gave the students nothing more than we had undertaken before the occupation began, but it sounded as if it did, so it was accepted by a Students' General Meeting on the 22nd March and by the College Council on the following day. Ten days later the term ended, when the occupying force would probably have gone home anyway.

I have recounted this incident in some detail as a period piece of the seventies, since I have not seen such a story told elsewhere. Looking back from the tough eighties to the guilt-ridden, angst-ridden seventies, from Mrs Thatcher's Britain to Mr Heath's, it looks easy: no chat, a quick Injunction, frogmarch the rebels out and send them down. But it is not easy to act out of period, or out of character. Either way, it was bound to leave a nasty taste, which was still in our mouths when the following year my tour of duty ended. By way of reconciliation C and I gave a series of drink parties in my room for staff and students of each school and department, but they tended to have the atmosphere of a sherry in the Headmaster's study, and the irreconcilables stayed away. The form taken by the political polarization of what used to be non-political institutions in our country, we can now see, is that there can be no reconciliation. The defeated, however fair and free the vote, swear vengeance and sulk in their tents. They no longer, like General von Blumentritt, put out a hand, even though theirs, like Brian Webb's, would be taken.

My departure was charmingly managed by my successor, Dick Guyatt. Nice things were said; beautifully crafted presents, in the highest traditions of the College, were most generously given. I left with joy, and though the place contains people I like a lot and miss, I have never wished to go back.

Defeats can also be escapes. This was another of those flights which go back through the years to summer afternoons when I would run out of the big house full of intelligent conversation into the haunted park. I was driven to these retreats from the pursuit of Fame partly in conscious reaction from early conditioning, partly in an unconscious gesture of self-protection. But this is still only half the story; for if it is true that my absurd haste to get out of London into the freedom and boredom of the country is a failure of nerve, it is also true that other flights have been in the opposite direction — into the action. We must do justice to our earlier selves: we owe them a certain loyalty, and I not least to that self to which Milton spoke with the matchless authority of his generation:

> I cannot praise a fugitive and cloistered virtue,
> that never sallies out and sees her adversary, but
> slinks out of the race when that immortal garland is
> to be run for, not without dust and heat.

Autobiography, which has to live uneasily between the secrets of the diary and the mask of the novel, is the art of the half-truth. It cannot for example tell the whole truth about either of the things that matter most in life — other people and the heart's affections — even if that platonic concept were attainable by us rather than laid up in Heaven. And the deepest springs of our own identity — our bodily attachment or non-attachment to the world — can only be hinted at. Nor is it just a matter of tactful selection — of steering a crafty course between superficiality and embarrassing confession. Much is hidden from us. Memory is selective, and we are all blindfolded by the instinct of self-protection. Beauty, by and large, seems a lot more accessible than truth — or is (as Keats might have put it) its most conspicuous manifestation. "Amazing, amazing," we keep exclaiming as we look around us. Pandora's box, if you look closer, contains a secret compartment, gleaming with jewels.

Appendix

CARACAS

31 July–7 August 1975

I HAVE SET out this report under four heads, and they are in order of priority in the sense that unless the earlier are implemented it will not be possible successfully to implement the later. They are:

A   Administration
B   Housing and Employment
C   Transportation
D   Quality of Life

A   Administration

1. Without exception, the officials whom I met agreed that the boundaries and powers of the Federal District authority ought now to be amended. At present Caracas is a very compact city with little commuting from beyond its green belt, but this pattern may change, and to allow for this and to ensure that the city has a strong tax base, it would probably be wise for the Federal District to comprise the metropolitan region itself (the region at present within the purview of the Municipal Office for Urban Planning (OMPU)) together with its green belt and the region beyond it in which satellite development is proposed. The present green belt has the character (but unfortunately not the authority) of an urban fence, which is supposed to delimit the expansion of the built-up area. It is manifestly *not* a green belt in the sense of a protected rural region on the far side of which satellite communities will be developed. It is for consideration whether it should be widened so as to fulfil this function.

2. My knowledge of Venezuelan administration is obviously inadequate for me to suggest what should be the hierarchy of powers within the new Federal District — for example whether it should be a two-level or a three-level structure. If there were to be three one would expect the top level (the Federal District itself) to be responsible for strategic land-use and transportation planning, housing and school building and major open spaces, the middle tier for development control, local road building, local parks, street lighting, sanitation, etc., and the lowest tier to be a means by which local communities could express their desires and their reactions to proposals affecting their daily lives.

3. But whatever the system, it seems to me wrong in principle that the powers of the city as planning authority should be limited by the existence of a number of central government agencies and public corporations (for example MOP, INAVI, CSB) which can in practice override its planning strategy. The master plan for Caracas is at present advisory and not mandatory. When it has been updated and accepted by the central government and all the City's constituent communities, it ought surely to have the force of law, and no development or construction agency ought to be able to overturn it. These agencies have remarkable and spectacular achievements to their credit. Their work could in future be equally spectacular, but better co-ordinated, if they operated within an agreed planning framework.

4. But also, whatever the system, it must be one that somehow ensures continuity through changes of government, without which planning is meaningless. It is sometimes wiser to persist in an existing policy because it is there, rather than to insist upon what looks like a better solution.

B   Housing and Employment

5. I have the strong impression that the imagination and expertise that have created the city's expressway system have not been applied to the even more important problem of housing, and it is a sign of this that a new agency (the Instituto Nacional de la Vivianda — INAVI) has now been set up with wider terms of reference. However, I am still not sure whether the right answer has been found.

6. Housing is not primarily a problem of production. It is a problem of planning. One may produce, or permit, thousands of dwellings, even well-designed ones, but they will be useless if there are no jobs for their owners, or if jobs involve too long or expensive a journey, or if junior schools and local shops and open spaces cannot be reached on foot. Of these relationships the most vital is that between housing and employment, which one has to try to keep in balance in terms of both numbers and location. For all these reasons it seems desirable that public housing and planning should be the work of the same authority. In the case of Caracas the relationship is a particularly critical one, because the decision has been taken (in my opinion rightly) that industrial growth shall not be permitted in the city, and an impressive organization has been set up by ODIPLAN to implement this policy by de-concentration and regional development. Caracas will remain the national capital, and its population will increasingly depend for employment on administrative jobs and servicing trades. Of course there will be substantial growth in these sources of employment, as in the past, but it will not be dramatic, and it seems a reasonable assumption that the natural increase of the existing population will be sufficient to take care of them.

7. In other words, the time has surely come to consider whether the

occupation of green-belt hillsides by immigrant squatters, with all the problems that this creates for future generations, could be brought to an end. Until this is done one can hardly blame other sections of the population (motorists for example) for treating the law with equal contempt. In 1941 Caracas had 56,000 people living in rancho dwellings; it now has 600,000 and the projection is that by 1990 it will have one million, a great many living at a density of 700 pph. Again, while in 1930 85 per cent of families lived in individual houses, it is projected that by 1990 85 per cent will live in multiple dwellings. These figures (if fulfilled) would reflect a tragic sacrifice of human happiness. I have been made well aware of the difficulties of enforcing a ban on non-authorized dwellings. In other Latin American countries it may be impossible and undesirable, but Venezuela's determination to apply so great a proportion of its resources to regional development must mean that she can now afford to climb out of this league.

8. This emphatically does not mean confining the city within the present green belt by putting the whole working population into high-rise tenements of the kind built in recent years. The gross population density of Caracas is three times that of an average European city. For obvious geographical reasons it will always be high, but an energetic policy of decongestion of people and jobs to new and expanded towns beyond the green belt, such as is at present proposed by OMPU, must be implemented, while for those whose jobs must remain within the city, new housing areas will need to be rapidly developed within the urban fence, either by renewal of obsolete parts of the western city or by planned extensions.

9. Meanwhile INAVI should become primarily an organization for housing research and development, with a particular concern in designing for steep slopes at fairly high density while providing easy access to the ground without the necessity for lifts (with their problems of vandalism and maintenance). The new designs should provide for both publicly built and self-built housing, and for a systematic programme of rancho improvement. Ninety per cent of Caracas housing may at present consist of high-rise flats or shacks, but examples do exist of better solutions. There are in Caricuao simple two-storey Mediterranean-style houses designed to cling to the hillside; there are a few pleasant "Radburn" type terrace houses in Coche; there are the European-scale flats of El Silencio (by the same architect). None of these meet all requirements: one has the feeling that the really imaginative architects the country possesses have not been attracted into this field, nor has research been done into relevant work in other countries, for example barrio improvement schemes in Lima and Bogota. There is much to be done if a future explosive situation is to be avoided.

10. I have referred to the need to keep housing and employment in balance in terms of both numbers and location. The second is of special importance in

Caracas in order to help reduce the overload on city transportation. Housing and workplaces and shops should be side by side, even in the same building, or at any rate within walking distance. Of course, people will often not take advantage of this but the facility should be there. Centro Simon Bolivar has set a grandiose example at Parque Central, and a similar mix of uses should be made obligatory in the case of all major renewal projects. This is one way in which housing agencies and private developers can contribute to the solution of the Caracas traffic crisis.

C   *Transportation*

11. In taking the courageous decision to make the great investment of the Metro project the Government evidently decided that there could be no question of moving the administrative capital elsewhere. The overriding necessity now is to push the project ahead with all possible speed, and to make certain that the city and the nation reap its full benefit, in terms of both economics and the quality of life. I will concentrate on these aspects.

12. Obviously it will be the policy to use every financial incentive to induce people to leave their cars at home and travel by metro. This will create a powerful attraction to build offices and flats as close as possible to the metro network, and a band of high land values about one kilometre wide along this network. It is of crucial importance that the benefit of these high land values should return to the state which created them. Undoubtedly the safest way to guarantee this is for the municipality to buy this land at existing use value and before speculators have moved in to force up its value. I understand that MOP have in fact been confined to buying land strictly necessary for engineering works, and that the intention is to recover the increment of value on adjacent sites by taxation and thereby to repay one third of the capital cost of the project. One can only hope that this method of recoupment will be equally effective. Certainly the world abounds with examples (including London) of failure to recoup this betterment for the community.

13. High charges for car use (to which I return later) will not in themselves be enough to ensure the necessary concentration of development along the metro network. They will need to be reinforced by planning restrictions. Planning permission for high density office development should not henceforth be given outside the one-kilometre band, so as to ensure that these high values are not dispersed in the intervening years. It will be equally important (again in order to avoid high traffic concentrations) to spread this development as evenly as possible along the band — and particularly to encourage it towards the extremities — and this also I return to later. By these means one ensures full and economic loading of the metro network and the minimum use of the overloaded road network.

14. I mention these things first under the head of transportation because

though they need immediate action they might be overlooked under the strain the road system will have to take over the next decade. This obviously needs no emphasis from me: it is the subject of a continuous stream of advice both professional and amateur. But it may help if I list briefly the armoury of weapons now available to fight the critical battle that lies ahead. There are two sides to it, increasing the capacity of the system and reducing the load it carries.

(a) Increasing the capacity of the system

15. Clearly some relief will be afforded by the completion of the Autopista Cota Mil (Avenida Boyaca) and by driving a new tunnel to the sea connected to new north-south freeways. And a number of obvious bottlenecks need attention. I understand that systematic evaluation of alternative transportation/land-use policies is in progress, but that the emphasis is likely to shift from new construction to better management of the existing system. In any case there is no need for delay in common sense measures like clearing all roads used by cross-town traffic of parked cars, imposing unilateral parking in minor streets, increasing one-way circulation, improving sidewalks and pedestrian crossings, prohibiting left turns, designing a large-scale street-marking system both vertical and horizontal to clarify all these restrictions, and above all setting up an effective force of traffic police with powers to levy on-the-spot fines. I am well aware that all these negative measures will be intensely disliked by Caracenos, who rightly pride themselves on their relaxed and considerate manners as drivers. One can only say that this is now an international language and no great city can get by without it.

16. The control of car-parking has now become a reasonably exact science. The ideal is to provide off-street parking financed both by private developers and by the proceeds of on-street parking charges. The number of car spaces needs to be carefully adjusted, since too few will force drivers into illegal kerbside parking, and too many will overload the roads that give access to them. Generally this adjustment is better done by experiment than by theory. Certainly there is *no* more effective way of increasing the capacity of the inner city road system.

(b) Reducing the load

17. Parking policy as above defined will itself have done a great deal to reduce overloading. It will need to be reinforced by two additional policies, one negative, one positive.

18. The negative policy is of course a campaign to control the number of cars brought into the city centre by imposing a special licence, or to limit their size by steeply progressive taxation on cubic capacity. Singapore, according to a recent report in the London *Times*, has recently introduced with apparent

success a scheme which offers motorists a variety of alternatives. I attach this report in an appendix, in case it may be of interest.

19. These or similar negative restrictions will only be tolerable and enforceable if the opportunity of the cleared streets is grasped to secure a dramatic improvement in the operating efficiency and the public image of the bus network. I know that a fleet of better buses has been introduced, and a specialist has been briefed to work out their progressive integration with the future metro system. His task is in fact more complex than this, and he will need a strong team to discharge it. A twofold integration is required, first with the road improvement and traffic management programme I have summarized, and secondly with the phased introduction of the metro. My own guess is that only a two-class bus system (hopefully as a temporary expedient) will persuade the middle classes to leave their cars at home. The present "normal" system must remain cheap, ruggedly designed and broadly deployed. The new "express" system must use softer vehicles, meticulously maintained, must run in special lanes, closed to cars, with priority at intersections, and must serve the main concentration of white-collar employment. It is impossible to exaggerate the urgency of this planning exercise, which need not be expensive to implement.

20. It must be realized that it will take the *whole* of this package of inter-dependent actions to achieve success. However, the final object of all this is not to enable machines to move about more rapidly, but to re-create a sense of joy for the human being on foot. To this I turn in the final section.

D   Quality of Life

21. One may wish to distribute development evenly along the metro network, but developers like sheep tend to flock together, and one must face the fact that the arrival of the metro in the Casco Central will release a flood of applications, held back hitherto by traffic congestion and shortage of parking space. This will be both a threat and an opportunity, and to confront it creatively it is urgent and essential that a plan for the historic heart of Caracas be prepared now. The closing of Plaza Bolivar to traffic has been a completely successful demonstration, and it is a question now not only of extending this as far as is practicable, but of ensuring that each block when rebuilt is comprehensively planned to include not only offices, flats, shops, etc., but also an internal pedestrian network completely separate from the traffic streets. The shopping arcades of Santiago, Chile, are an interesting nineteenth-century precedent.

22. The inner core of the colonial city, which contains the main national monuments, is bounded by the Panteon Nacional to the north, and by the Avenidas Beralt, Bolivar and Fuerzas Armadas. The aim, if attainable, should be to exclude through traffic from this area and to prepare for it a

three-dimensional model which will safeguard the small scale of its historic buildings and open spaces. For example the surroundings of the Panteon Nacional have become a national scandal, and the same applies to much of the La Pastora area. Within this inner core no demolition should be permitted without approval, and new buildings should be in sympathy with the old in scale and character. Wherever space exists for them, trees should be planted.

23. To the south of Avenida Bolivar and in Catia large-scale renewal should be encouraged within the general policies recommended in earlier sections. Buildings in these areas will go high. As a contrast, the whole of the great space adjacent to the Avenida Bolivar should be kept open, and designs should immediately be commissioned to transform it into the centre of the city's life and pleasure. The "paseo" seems to have vanished from Caraceno life, which makes it at sunset as dull for visitors as any North American city. This great space could provide for parking underground and for a surface of varying levels with water features, plenty of shade, generous planting, open-air shows, art exhibitions and every kind of public amusement. Avenida Bolivar itself would, of course, be spanned by wide pedestrian bridges, perhaps bordered by little shops.

24. A similar but more difficult challenge is presented by the commercial centre of Sabana Grande, where the collision between vehicles and pedestrians is at its most brutal. It is more difficult because the opportunity was lost, when it was extensively developed in recent years, to place all shops and accesses to buildings on a pedestrian deck above the traffic. However the challenge must be accepted and a civilized pedestrian network somehow contrived for this great and growing centre. Perhaps the closure of Avenida Abraham Lincoln (like Oxford Street, London) to all traffic except buses and taxis, and the doubling in width of its sidewalks, would be a good start.

25. These two great pedestrian centres could then become the twin nodes of a great web of pedestrian and cycle routes covering the entire city. To insert this web into a motorized city, by threading together every quiet shady street, every neglected river or stream, every narrow alley, every public open space, and of course by creating new small public gardens and playspaces, will be a fascinating and rewarding undertaking.

26. All the same, people will always want to escape from this high-density city at weekends, not only to the sea, but into the wild interior. A great deal more could be done to make the so-called green belt a beautiful and usable landscape: for a start, all commercial advertising hoardings should be removed from it. I would also suggest that the Environment Commission set up a small department to define and administer a number of camp sites and picnic areas in the National Parks and in other areas of natural landscape. These could be used by the schools to teach a new generation an

understanding and affection for the trees and plants that will fill the Caracas of the future.

27. This city, with its magnificent setting and climate, and its brilliant artists and architects (whose imagination it has shown it knows how to use) could become one of the great tourist cities: at the moment one cannot even buy a set of postcards made by an imaginative photographer.

★

28. I have tried in this report to concentrate on immediate action, while having constantly in mind that this action must be consistent with the findings of more long-term and systematic investigations. I am well aware that most of what I have written will be very familiar to my colleagues in Caracas, who will know, as I do, how much easier it is to propose than to execute. But I am equally aware of a strong determination on the part of the Governor that what is necessary for the well-being of the people of Caracas will be done. I would like to thank him for the kindness with which he received me, and all the officials who gave their time to our conversations, and particularly to mention my colleague, Gonzalo Castellanos, who accompanied me throughout and provided the excellent record on which I have based this report.

AUGUST 1975   ESHER

INDEX